I0429453

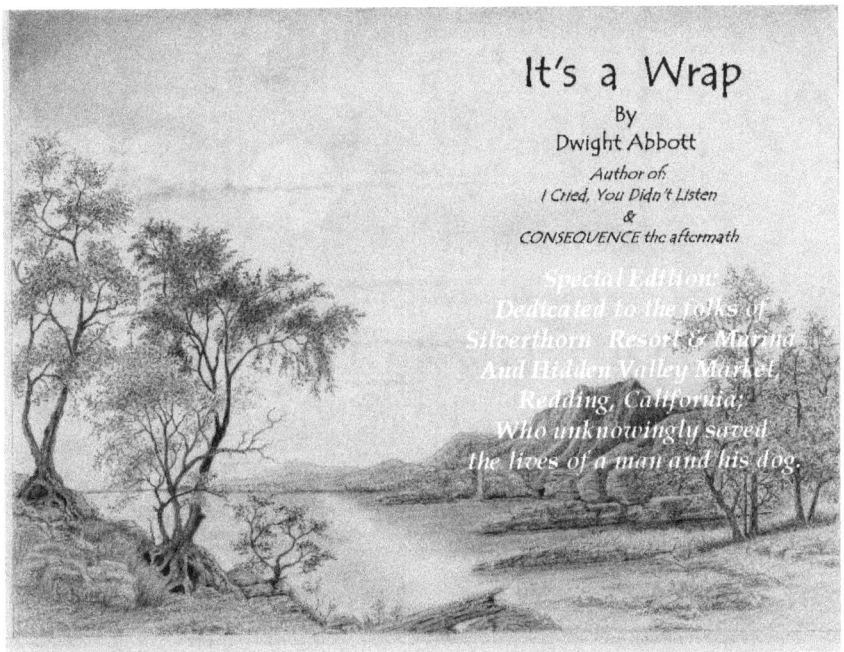

It's a Wrap
By
Dwight Abbott
Author of:
I Cried, You Didn't Listen
&
CONSEQUENCE the aftermath

Special Edition:
Dedicated to the folks of
Silverthorn Resort & Marina
And Hidden Valley Market
Redding, California;
Who unknowingly saved
the lives of a man and his dog.

ABOUT THE BOOK COVER

Artwork By Dwight Abbott; November 24, 2009

This morning, I sat to draw for you, a place I often went to - near you; yet, just outside of Redding - when I was being hunted; a place I knew well enough I felt safe there; where I could be alone; a place I was convinced I would be allowed to lick my wounds, to die if necessary: Silverthorn Resort; Jones Valley. Imagine me there, Skippy, straddling the fallen log, looking out over my domain, rifle ready propped nearby. Where I cooked food from my often meager supplies on the tip of land forming the inlet to your right. At night I would roll out my sleeping bag to sleep near the dying embers. Free for a moment.   *Dwight Abbott*

Silverthorn Resort and Marina

Silverthorn Marina, as seen from Silverthorn
Resort and Restaurant
16250 Silverthorn Rd. Redding CA. 96007
800-332-3044; 530-275-1571

Hidden Valley Market

Hidden Valley Country Store
22009 Hidden Valley Dr.
Redding, California 96003
530-275-1102

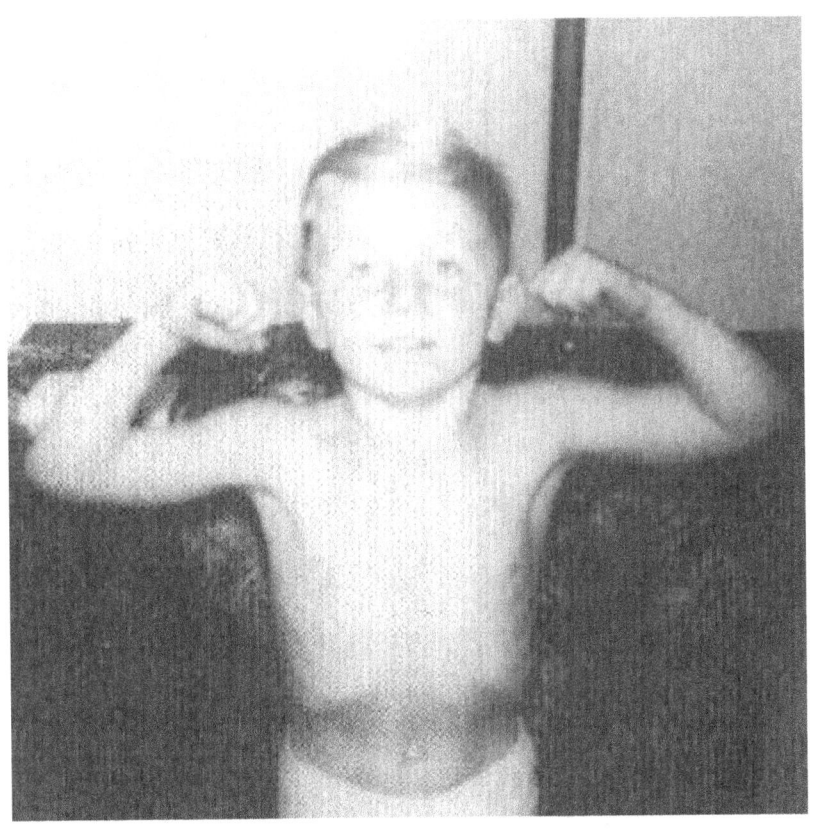

Sonny; Durfee Blvd, El Monte, California 1949

Sonny combing Moms Hair

I Cried, You Didn't Listen

Danny and Dwight Abbott, 9 years old.

I AM SONNY

It's a Wrap!

Dwight Edgar Abbott

DEDICATION

For those who, without many hours of work;
My books would not exist!
Karren Killian; Helpmate & Editor
Michael Kroll; Friend & Commentator
Danny Abbott; Brother & Publisher
Terry Abbott; Sister in Law & Confidant.
[see end of book]

CONTENTS

ACKNOWLEDGMENTS

Jeff Palin & Silverthorn Resort
Wendy of Hidden Valley Market
Karren Killian; Michael Kroll;
Raymond Cooper; Danny Abbott;
Terry Abbott; Loretta Gumabo;
Larry Gumabo;
Tommy
Popcorn; Oatmeal & Sate

CHRISTMAS MEMORIES

I believe it was 1976, but don't quote me on that. My girlfriend and I were living inside my van with our dog. Meandering around Shasta County, up in Northern California, we met some folks who had set up a Christmas Tree lot South of Redding, along Hilltop Drive. Vividly I remember bright colorful lights, the smell of freshly cut Oregon trees, sawdust spread thickly over the ground. For several weeks through December, Mary Ann and I, and, of course our dog, were invited to gather there around a large metal drum in which a fire had been set, where together with them we sang songs and shared laughter.

Christmas Eve, the lot abandoned; once proud trees left to wither, Mary Ann and I returned to warm ourselves over a fire we rekindled. From the surrounding gloom we carried into the light a tree to decorate with ornaments earlier broken and left strewn.

Shortly after midnight we exchanged gifts. I had for her matching checkered wool mittens and scarf. She, a Timex watch for me. Not fifty cents between us.....neither asked 'how?' Just like in the movies, it began to snow. Hugging one another, Mary Ann began to softly hum "Silent Night." Sate (short for Satan), jumped into the back of the van. We may not have had fifty cents, but that early morning I was the wealthiest man in town.

Each Christmas this finds its way into my head, moving me to wish I could have it 'just one more time.' Unfortunately, serving four consecutive life sentences, that is not going to happen. But I can dream it.

Is there Christmas here where I exist? After all, it feels like just another day. Inside the cell block there is no tree with colorful flashing lights, no music, no chaplain walking the tiers occasionally stopping to share what he believes it is all about. Very few of us are reminded it is some sort of 'special day' only because family and friends traveled here to share, for hours, with us in the Visiting Room. There we can appreciate the efforts to put up decorations in the far corner of the room, around a tree set atop a table. Below the tree a child plays with toys that the prisoners purchased for them.

On a long ago Christmas Day, I received a visit. Each time I looked across the room to the tree, and beautifully wrapped spurious gifts, I found it was being ignored. Not by me! By the time I left the Visiting room several stems from the tree, along with a small handful of tinsel, were hidden away in my wheelchair. Upon returning to my cage I gave what I had taken to Raymond, my cell mate. He smiled and smelled them; it had also been a very long time for him.

While I slept soundly through the night; Raymond, with considerable attention to detail, painstakingly taped and glued the stems, I had given him; together to shape a tiny tree, after which, he pushed the bare bottom of the stalk into an unopened Top Ramen Soup, for a foundation. He then hung the tinsel.

I awakened Christmas morning to discover the tree, and underneath it something wrapped in pages torn from a magazine. With a red marking pen Ray had 'borrowed' from a guard, he wrote: "To Sonny from Raymond; merry Christmas Old Man." Inside was a CD; "The Eagles, Their Greatest Hits". One of only three CDs he had, I knew he coveted it, not having a whole lot. He refused to loan it to anyone who asked, other than me, and had several times refused to sell it.

I knew he would nap, after having been awake most of the night; I waited. The only thing I had that he knew meant anything to me was my sunglasses. He borrowed them every time he left the cell alone, even if he was going only to the dimly lit Dayroom. I was never without them when I was outside. We called them my 'paranoid glasses'.

Later that afternoon, knowing how much I liked those glasses, my loyal friend tried to refuse them. Though now in different prisons, I still have the CD, and he the glasses.

DWIGHT (SONNY) & DANNY (SKIPPY) ABBOTT
SALINAS VALLEY STATE PRISON; AUGUST 22, 2010
BROTHERS STILL.....!

"The Glasses!"

PAROLE:
A PARODY

In the eschewing minutes, hours, and day, when I first walked through the doors, upon my release from prison, after 36 years of incarceration; I rapidly concluded the strange looking device clipped to everyone's belt was some sort of status symbol. Each time it emitted a beeping sound, all around me, men and women, would stop whatever they were doing, grab-up the devices, hold it near their faces, and peer at it. Apparently when satisfied it was still there, they would discreetly look around, appearing to assure themselves all had seen they did this thing before returning it to their belts and continuing with whatever activity they had been performing when interrupted.

Financially embarrassed, I was unable to purchase whatever this was that made the ladies look-on with admiration and respect. I was dispirited. You might imagine my excitement and pride as I left a Salvation Army Thrift Store, head held high, and strapped to my belt....you guessed it, a garage door opener. My pride and joy knew no bounds.

Prominently hanging from the strings holding up my pants, where I could comfortably reach for it every thirty seconds or so to give it a good look, I swaggered to Highway 17, stuck out my thumb at the bottom of an off-ramp and hitched a ride out of San Jose to Los Gatos, California where everyone, excepting myself, suffers from an over-abundance of wealth.

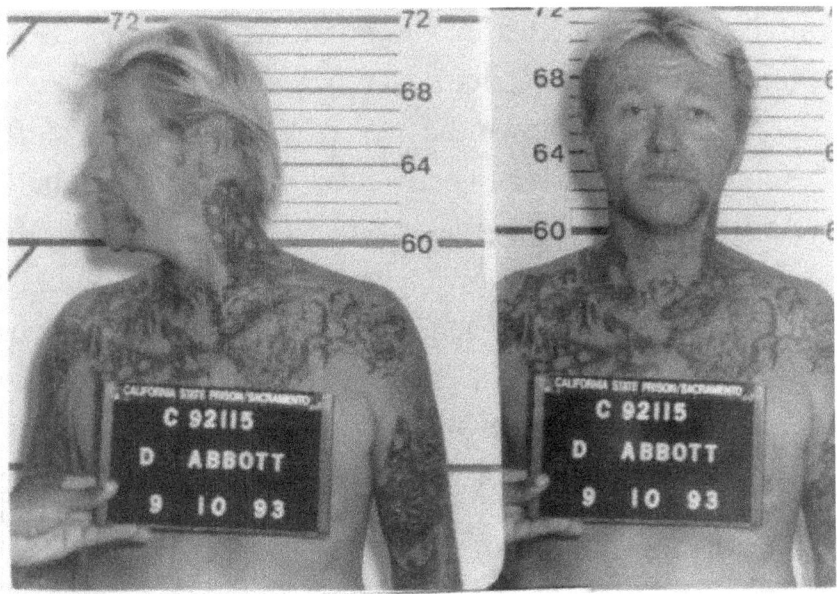

Complementing the extensive prison artwork tattooed over my body, I smoothed the wrinkles from my muscle-man T-shirt, while swatting the fine gray dust off after stepping down from the cement truck. Immediately I noticed fellow citizens shying from me. At first I thought it was my intimidating manliness; that is, before lifting my arm and sniffing around there. I shoplifted a small fortune in different brands of deodorant to no avail. They still stepped away.

"Ah," it came to me, it was the bright fluorescent orange flip-flops generously given me, by a guard, when I paroled that morning; obviously causing me to appear a bit of a snob. Immediately I removed both from my feet and placed them inside a small brown paper lunch bag I had filled with my worldly possessions at the prison, after eating the bologna sandwich one of the other convicts had swiped from the guard who was distracted signing my release papers.

I continued on down the sidewalk, strutting my stuff, wishing I did not have to carry the conspicuous bag, but I would need the slippers later when I had to get dressed up for job interviews. The teacher of my pre-release class at San Quentin Prison had confided, "First impressions will be a major factor in the decision making process, in whether or not you get the job". I had committed that advice to memory, word-for-word, and was confident the flip-flops would be noticed by the interviewer.

I sensed I was beginning to fit in with the large crowd out enjoying the hot, sunny day. I must confess to feeling just a wee bit out of place while hopping down the main street, unsuccessfully keeping the bare soles of my feet off the concrete, heated by the 106 degree weather. No matter. I was not one to easily surrender. Encouraging me were the admiring glances directed my way by the many beautiful, pleasingly clad ladies, as I stood in a warm puddle of water cooling myself. Their coy manner made it obvious it had been a while, if ever, since they were able to appreciate such raw, gorgeous masculinity. It was obvious they wanted, no.....'needed' me.

Near mid-town, I arrived at a small, quaint public park, where I first sensed my shyness working against me. I burst loose from those shackles and approached three beautiful women standing together in conversation. Immediately I noticed their necks bow as they bashfully looked down and away, smiles ever so slight forming upon their lips that were undoubtedly longing for mine. They knew not how to address this hunk of a man who has taken their breath away.

It seemed prudent to step away, allow the three to compose themselves, to gather their thoughts. I moved over to a nearby water fountain and drank from it, all the while discreetly watching the ladies watching me. I thought nothing of the fact that it was dusky, tasted a bit odd, a little gritty on the tongue, just like prison. I did not notice the printed warning affixed to the faucet: "CONTAMINATED! DO NOT DRINK THIS WATER!"

It was then I heard muffled giggling as one of the ladies spoke: "I think I saw him on the 'Worlds dumbest Criminals'." That really pissed me off because my Parole Officer had not informed me my criminal history had been televised.

Not one to be discouraged by these things, I returned to my outlaw lifestyle, knowing that shortly after my 'Most Wanted' mug shot (hoping it was one of the better one's snapped during one of my many bookings) would again adorn walls of Post Offices all over the country, where women would surely admire them, wishing I would soon be captured so that they could write to me and get permission to visit with me. Shhhh....don't tell anyone about this. I do not want the other guys to butt in on my action.

BILLY

When dad came home from another busy and trying day, we usually hid to avoid being told, or shamed, to work on a particular chore agreed upon the day before. Yet today was different. Dad paid little, if any, attention to us, said nothing that once again we were hard at work doing nothing. Lost in thought, he stared right through us.

When we asked to go over to our neighbors house and play with the boys there, dad replied, "No, we have something to do today."

Our hearts sank. Usually when dad said ".....something to do" we knew it meant work, and lots of it. "Darn! We should have been outside doing something"

I remember thinking.

Holding our collective breaths, fearing upon learning what the task was going to be we would feel 'another' cardiac arrest coming on, it was I, the not so bright one, who asked, "What is it we are going to do?"

"We are going for a drive."

Inside the shiny, nearly new Plymouth, nobody spoke. Sitting still on the large back seat, not arguing and fighting was a first for us kids. Dad seemed to be in a trance as he drove east of our home in Covina, California toward San Bernardino. Often we went this way to go target shooting out in the desert, but this time we had not brought the .22 rifles.

We went by our usual turn off into the desert. A short while later Dad turned onto an unfamiliar sandy road that obviously had not been used for a very long time. The heavy car drove over sagebrush, cacti and small Yucca trees. Sadly, there were a couple of bunny rabbits Daddy tried to avoid, but didn't. Winding into the distance, this road appeared to be without end.

After what seemed a hundred miles, a form loomed ahead, obviously, to us, not a Yucca tree. At first we thought it was another mirage, then it began to take shape. Boulders, large and small, round and flat. Once past the tricks the desert will play on its visitors, a ramshackle cabin appeared set upon and isolated knoll.

Its wood was bleached and splintered. What once was a door, now leaned haphazardly against a rock, its tattered leather hinges slowly being eaten up by the elements. For a moment my interest was drawn to the dozen of lizards crawling up and over the door, until I caught movement elsewhere. Sun-bleached cloth hanging from what once was the cabin's only window fluttered in the gentle wind. The roof was sinking down to lean in such a way that the day would soon arrive when the cabin would collapse and disappear forever. Cans and bottles were laying about.

Dad brought the car to a halt aside the shack. In silence we all sat looking. I seemed to recognize this place, certainly sensed it to be 'Sacred Ground.' Then from Daddy there came a long buried memory, the first and last story of his childhood we would ever hear.

(From here I will rely on my brother's memory of what was said)

"I was raised in orphanages my entire life. My only family became, and was, those boys I shared the different homes and experiences with. The last orphanage I was in was "Boys Town." I was 13 years old at the time and had long before lost count of the many institutions I had been in.

"For almost a year I had managed to remain friends with an older boy named Billy. I regret I do not remember, nor do I know if I ever did know, his last name. I believe he was around 15. Not one of us really knew our ages, as birthday celebrations simply did not happen.

"We were never happy at any of the orphanages. Many abuses, or perceived abuses, occurred. None of us really cared. If any did, they were certainly outnumbered by those who did not. Memories of real parents or siblings were non-existent. We were constantly obsessed with scheming to escape to somewhere, anywhere but were we were at."

"Billy was pretty much the leader, and I the follower." (That was hard for Skippy and I to imagine, as our dad had always been the strongest human being we had ever known.)

"One afternoon," dad continued, "Billy called me over to tell me he was leaving. I asked him what he planned. Billy pointed out that the night matron would do bed checks in the early evening and that was when he was going out the front door. He wanted me to go with him, not that I had to be asked. It sounded really easy. I did not stop to think that the door might be kept locked, much less what would happen once we were out. Billy was the only brother I had ever known, and never did I doubt his judgment."

Daddy seemed about to lose himself in another time as he stared to the distant mountains.

"That night, moving the cleaning supplies around, Billy and I hid in the hallway closet. It was there we waited for the matron to walk past the cracked closet door and enter the dormitory. At the sound of its door swinging shut, Billy pushed open the closet door, and out we ran to the matron's temporarily abandoned desk."

The front door consisted of a steel frame enclosing thick glass, secured with a heavy duty double lock. Billy disappeared behind the desk and returned carrying a baseball bat. I was surprised when he told me we were going through the window, further making it clear we would have no second chance. We would have to give it everything we could the first time.

"Without hesitation, we stepped back about twenty feet. With me behind him, my friend raised the bat and we ran toward the window with me against his back. Obviously we were going to go through that window or die trying. There was a loud sound of breaking glass and a few seconds later, with me atop Billy, we were lying in a pile of broken glass outside on the front walk. We had done it, no matter the noise made was enough to wake the dead."

"Quickly, we caught our breath, regained our senses, stood, and bolted into the darkness. Tripping and stumbling, we ran, until we could run no longer; stopping to rest but only for a moment. It was to be a long night ahead of us. Finally we stopped to sleep on the ground, where we frequently wakened to the slights sounds.

"The next day, and several after, we continued our trek, doing the best two slight boys can do to put as much distance between them and that home. Occasionally wandering near houses, we stole clothes, bedding, begged food and rides. Somehow Billy always made sure I was warm, my stomach full, or close to it as possible under the circumstances. Surprising him, and myself, I was able to keep up. Our plan was 'distance', and somehow we ended in this cabin, abandoned even then, when it seemed to be in good shape."

With an explosion of confusion, one of us asked:
"Do you mean you and Billy where here when you

were little boys?"

"Yes."

"Did you stay here? How long? Where did you go after?"

"We remained a week, maybe ten days, no more."

"Where did you go?"

"I eventually made it to Los Angeles."

"Huh? What about Billy?"

Daddy paused, then stared, his hand against his chest as if he were in pain.

"Billy stayed here."

"What? Why didn't you go together?"

"We couldn't."

We became alarmed. 'Why couldn't they stay together? Were they not brothers? Did they not need each other? Did they have to run from someone or 'something'; and get split up, not finding one another after? Did he ever find Billy?' Questions that screamed to be asked aloud; yet remained silent.

Dad opened the car door, slowly got out and began to walk toward the side of the shed, all the while looking down at the ground. Mutely we followed along the narrow, barely visible footpath now behind the shed. No one spoke. Somehow we knew that the revealing of a great mystery, and answers to the questions we had, lie just ahead, at the end of this overgrown path.

Reaching the end, where there was a scattering of more old, bleached boards, among a pile of rounded rocks about the size of baseballs, and drying grasses growing through the cracks. Daddy stared at the pile of rocks. We stared at him, unable to believe our eyes. Dad was crying. The lumps in our throats kept us from saying anything as we found ourselves struggling with tears escaping from our own eyes. Skippy and I stood beside one another watching dad as he began to carefully move aside a small family of cacti still with their leaves and the accumulations of sagebrush plants brought there by shifting sands. The sand was soft, our dad strong. His arms rippled with strength and determination as these things gave way in his grasp.

The covering removed, and more of the ground came

into view, we realized the rocks were beginning to form some sort of pattern. Dad stepped back, leaving us to stare at what he had uncovered. There upon the ground was a cross.

My throat dried and I was finding it difficult to catch my breath. Now we knew. Any doubts were being wiped from our minds while the dry wind tousled our hair.

"This was the cabin's privy," Daddy began again. "It was no longer used, hadn't been for many years far as I could tell. It was just a hole. I placed Billy's body into it, filled it with sand and covered it with rocks. After it was sealed; best I could; I made this cross, as that seemed the thing to do, even if God had abandoned us.

"After discovering this shack Billy decided we would hide out here, lay low for awhile. It had been raining for several hours when we again spread our stolen bedding inside the cabin and immediately went to sleep. After a couple of days the rains stopped and finally I began to warm. The cabin was built on a rock outcropping. The rocks warmed quickly and held their heat, keeping us warm through the nights and early mornings."

"Early one morning Billy awakened me screaming, terror in his voice. I began to get up and he held me down. 'Don't move', he yelled; 'Rattlesnakes everywhere!' He and I began to cry.

In a struggling voice he told me to stand and lay over his shoulders when he bent over. More scared than I had ever been before, I did just as he asked. He stood and began to carry me outside, where after a while he laid me down on the sand. Strangely, I had not seen any rattlesnakes. Billy fell down beside me, no doubt exhausted. He began to strip off his clothing, crying in pain. Understanding, I tried to help. He told me he'd been bitten on his feet several times, and once that he knew of, on his neck. He told me the bites felt like the worst wasp sting he'd ever felt. I began to hope that's all they were; wasp stings. His eyes began to dart to and fro, and he was sweating; yet shivered violently, as if very cold.

"As I tried to wipe clean his wounds they were swelling before my eyes. Billy was in considerable pain. I did not understand 'shock'. Billy began to shake and salivate. His breathing became labored. Before he passed out and became still, he made very little sense as he tried to talk. I thought he had gone to sleep and held him in my arms. Billy never woke up."

"It took me a while to figure it out, but we had been laying our blankets on a nest of rattlesnakes deep in the rocks. It was the movement or warmth of our bodies that drew them up to the surface. After I buried Billy I killed every snake I could find. Afterward, I grabbed whatever I felt safe grabbing, knowing I had to leave before the rattlesnakes reappeared."

To this time I have never felt what I felt for Dad that day as he turned and walked towards the car. I wanted to hug him, tell him I was sorry for his friend. The three of us got into the car where the sadness smothered me.

In silence, each of our minds were busy going over the events of that day, life's lessons. We were awfully young, but we had learned the true definition of love. We knew Billy had given his life to save that of his friend, our father. There were no words that could be spoken that afternoon that would not seem to cheapen Billy's sacrifice.

"Love?" On a desert hill above the Willow Creek Campground, south of Hoover Dam on the Arizona side, covered with sagebrush, cacti and Yucca trees Dad leaped between my little brother and a very angry rattlesnake, the while undoubtedly knowing he would be bitten instead of my little brother. As Skippy has written, that's another story.

("Love?" Read about Donald "Stubby" Stubblefield in I Cried, You Didn't Listen, 2014 by Dwight Abbott. Available at Amazon.com, Barnes and Noble and CreateSpace).

Dwight Abbott (wight): "I handle 'em' with gloves for they are growing now and chew my fingers all up"

Sonny's Family

Read about Sonny's return from the Optimist Home for Boys in Chapter 5 of "I Cried, You Didn't Listen." With his Family: 1955; 13 years old. 7326 Nestle Ave, Reseda Ca. Danny (Skippy); halfsister, Carolyn J. Scott; half brother, David L. Scott; mother, Betty; Dwight (Sonny); dad, Dwight Sr.

Abbott home on Stillwater Creek .3 miles west to Old Oregon Trail .5 Miles South to old Hwy 44. Danny built his first snowman here.

Dwight Edgar "Sonny" Abbott

Dwight Ellsworth Abbott CCC (affectionately: " wight")

Stillwater

Abbott Turkeys Stillwater Creek Redding, Cal Circa 1950

DWIGHT AND DWIGHT
GO AWOL!

Written By:

Dwight Abbott & Danny Abbott

The hardest part of our stories may be getting beyond disbelief; but, it is all true. Terry, Dwight Abbott the II; and Danny were with Sonny, as he was Captured in an 'no shots fired' gun battle showdown; when Swat teams; guns drawn; surrounded our home. It seems that, when one is looking down the barrels of a dozen automatic weapons; YOU BELIEVE!!

Skippy and I ARE "Story Tellers"; not simply to 'Entertain; but, because we BELIEVE that the truth should be known for those who follow; that they may avoid the same MISTAKES and wrong turns!.

Escaping Prisons; run in The Abbott Family!

Following the recent death of the last known living participant in our Dad's (Dwight Elsworth Abbott) infamous escape from Folsom Prison in 1932; Skippy and myself are considering releasing [In **Fifth Edition** of <u>"I Cried, You Didn't Listen"</u> and <u>"CONSEQUENCE the aftermath"</u>] the full story of his escape and how he avoided capture for the rest of his life.

It is truly a Fascinating and Enthralling Story. A movie made in the seventies used our Dad's original escape techniques for "drama". It was in those years that Dad, finally confided, in several " hypothetical third person" discussions with Skippy and I; an almost unbelievable story of intrigue and danger. Forever more; The story of Dad "Looking over his shoulder" and keeping his "secret", while raising a family of curious teens; even to his grave, is, in itself, beyond amazing.

Larger text

follows these

News

Clippings.

**OAKLAND TRIBUNE
JUNE 17, 1932**

DWIGHTS DAD,
DWIGHT ELSWORTH ABBOTT
ESCAPES FOLSOM PRISON
LEAVING BEHIND
A PAPER MACHE "DUMMY"!
ABBOTT WAS NEVER CAPTURED.
HIS DARING AND CLEVER
ESCAPE LATER BEING
MADE INTO THE MOVIE:

"ESCAPE
FROM
ALCATRAZ"

WHEN SONNY AND I
WERE FINALLY TOLD,
BY DAD, HOW HE
WAS ABLE TO STAY
A FREE MAN,
HE SHARED A
FASCINATING; YET
ENTHRALLING TALE!
READ EDITION 5 !

CONVICT PUTS DUMMY IN BED AND ESCAPES

Los Angeles Robber Plays Clever Trick to Get Out of Folsom: Still at Large

FOLSOM PRISON, June 17.— Using a clever dummy to hide his escape, Dwight E. Abbott, 24, Los Angeles robber, was still missing from Folsom prison today, after a 24-hour hunt revealed only scant traces of the prisoner.

Abbott's ruse was discovered yesterday after the morning check-up. Prison guards then discovered the dummy in Abbott's bunk, and the cellmates of the missing man, Fred Shamblin, 37, and Wallace Sabin, 21, both sentenced from Los Angeles, were questioned.

ADMITS HIS PART.

Sabin, Warden Court Smith said, freely admitted his part in the escape, claiming he and Abbott committed various minor infractions of prison rules to assure they would be locked in the cell all day Sunday.

It was then the men prepared the dummy which they completed even to hair which Sabin had asked the prison barbers to clip from his head "because of dandruff."

HIDES OUT ALL NIGHT.

Abbott apparently hid out Wednesday night, escaped over the wall with a rope made of bed ticking, stole a car belonging to a Folsom resident and headed for Sacramento. The automobile was abandoned a few miles from town when it ran out of gasoline.

Shamblin, the other cell mate, although knowing of the escape, apparently played no part in helping Abbott, prison officials believe.

Oakland Tribune, June 17 1932

Commentary by Danny:

Dwight's Dad' Dwight Elsworth Abbott, Escaped Folsom Prison, on June 17, 1932.. He Left behind a Paper Mache Dummy.

Hard as it is to believe, he was never "captured". His daring and Clever escape was later copied and became script for the Movie:

"Escape from Alcatraz".

When Sonny and I, were finally told by Dad, how he was able to remain a "free man"; he shared a Fascinating; yet, Enthralling Tale of Adventure, as a "Fugitive" from justice!

We are preparing the story for inclusion in our next Edition 5, of:

"CONSEQUENCE the aftermath".

Los Angeles Times; May 7, 1931

NOT HANDCUFFED

As Abbott was standing in the hallway just after recess had been ordered by Superior Judge Willis, presiding at the trial at which the prisoner had just testified, Deputy Sheriff West ordered him to stick out his hands to be handcuffed. It is contrary to law to take a man into court shackled.

Instead of extending his hands, Abbott placed them on a railing, and vaulted to the iron floor of the stairway landing, ten feet below. Deputy Sheriffs West and Roberts drew their revolvers, but a crowd of women jurors was standing on the stairway, and the officers could not take the risk of shooting. Bailiff Arthur Shivell, in Judge Willis's court, who brought back a sharpshooter's medal from overseas twelve years ago, drew a bead on the fleeing convict, but an excited woman blundering into the field of fire probably saved Abbott's life.

The prisoner ran down the front steps of the Courthouse and turned south toward the Hall of Records. Bailiff Lunkin from Department 10 meanwhile had drawn his pistol, and with several bystanders joined the chase.

Diagram by Times Staff Artist Phil Leonard of Exciting Race and Insets of Fugitive and

SALESMAN ALERT

One of the bystanders who took up the pursuit was Reidy, a real estate salesman, who ran through the Hall of Records and east down an alley to New High street. Meanwhile the deputies were pursuing their quarry across a bridge from the Hall of Records into an annex where offices of the County Planning Commission are located.

Reidy saw the fugitive raise a window and hang from the sill. The man released his hold and dropped twenty-five feet to the pavement and, stunned by the fall, seemed unable to rise. Reidy pounced on him and held him until Bailiffs Lunkin and Shivell ran up with their handcuffs.

In the courtroom after the chase, Abbott, excused by Judge Willis and ordered back to the penitentiary, protested that he was in great pain and could not walk over to the jail.

TAKEN TO JAIL

"If you could run that fast, you can certainly walk," said Deputy Sheriff West, jerking the prisoner to his feet, and hauling him across to the jail.

In the jail hospital, Abbott was examined by Dr. Blank, who said an X-ray would be necessary to determine whether the prisoner's back, or his legs, are broken.

After recess Judge Willis admonished the jury not to permit the knowledge of Abbott's attempt to escape to influence their deliberations in the case of Charles Lee Quinn and Roy Vernon Quinn, whose second trial for the robbery of the Lotus Cafe in Pasadena is nearing its close.

Abbott had been brought from Folsom by Attorney C. J. Orbison, for the defense, and testified that he and not the Quinn brothers held up the cafe May 28, 1930, and robbed Robert Mullins, the proprietor, of $135.

Although witnesses in the cafe identified the Quinns, four police officers from the Lincoln Heights jail testified that Roy Quinn was a prisoner at the time of the robbery. Dep. Dist. Atty. Patton, prosecuting, argued that Roy, being a trusty, might have left the jail long enough to commit the robbery.

Abbott was in the County Jail awaiting trial for robbery when he met the Quinn boys and there, they say, confessed to the crime of which they were accused. Later Abbott was brought back from Folsom, where he subsequently had been sentenced to a life term as a habitual criminal, and testified at the first trial of the Quinns. A conviction had at this trial was reversed and a new trial ordered.

Attorneys probably will conclude argument at today's session of the trial and the case will go to the jury.

Dwight Elsworth Abbott
continued from previous page
Los Angeles Times May 7, 1931. Page A2

Felon Escapes From California Prison

FOLSOM PRISON, Calif., June 16.—(UP)—Dwight E. Abbott, 24, Los Angeles robber, escaped from Folsom prison last night, and his absence was not discovered until the general lock-up late today, prison officials said.

Warden Court Smith discovered Abbott had made a dummy with a plaster of paris face, adorned with real hair cut from the heads of himself and his cellmate. The dummy, seen in his bed, was lifelike enough to deceive guards.

Dad Escaped from Folsom
about a Year after his attempted escape from
The Los Angeles Courthouse

Reno Nevada Gazette
June 16, 1932

Los Angeles Times; May 7, 1931

THE SAN BERNADINO COUNTY SUN
NOVEMBER 28, 1976

ESCAPE — Dwight Edgar Abbott II, 34, of Soledad State Prison. Charged with escape from state prison. Pleaded guilty as charged. Sentence to state prison suspended, ordered to serve one year in county jail with credit for 124 days already

READ THE FULL STORY OF DWIGHT'S ESCAPE FROM SOLEDAD STATE PRISON IN EDITION 5 OF "I CRIED, YOU DIDN'T LISTEN" OR "CONSEQUENCE THE AFTERMATH!

THE AMARILLO GLOBE TIMES JULY 20, 1960

READ THE FULL STORY OF SONNY'S ESCAPE FROM THE DUMAS COUNTY JAIL IN EDITION 5 OF "I CRIED, YOU DIDN'T LISTEN" OR "CONSEQUENCE THE AFTERMATH"

Man Escapes Dumas Jail

DUMAS, July 20 (Special) — Moore County officers and Dumas police continued their search today for a pipeline worker who escaped from the Dumas jail through an air shaft about 4 p.m. Tuesday, although no new developments had been reported in the search this morning.

The worker was arrested for creating a disturbance and for investigation in connection with another offense. He is Dwight Edgar Abbott, 21.

Police first learned of the escape, according to Dumas Police Chief Frank Hudson, when a man in the apartment house where Abbott had been living reported the escapee had rushed into his apartment for a butcher knife and then left.

Abbott was described as about 6 feet tall, weighing about 175 pounds and wearing a duck-tail haircut. His hair is a straw brown.

ESCAPE FROM ~~ALCATRAZ~~

FOLSOM

TRIBUNE TEXT:

FOLSOM PRISON, June 17, 1932 –

Los Angeles Robber Plays Clever Trick to Get Out Of Folsom; Still at Large

Using a clever dummy to hide his escape, Dwight E. Abbott, 24, Los Angeles robber was still missing from Folsom prison today, after a 24 - hour hunt revealed only scant traces of the prisoner. Abbott's ruse was discoverer yesterday after the morning checkup.

Prison guards then discovered the dummy in Abbotts' bunk, and the cell mates of the missing man Fred Schamblin,37, and Wallace Sabin, 21, both sentenced from Los Angeles, were questioned.

ADMITS HIS PART.

Sabin, Warden Court Smith said, freely admitted his part in the escape, claiming he and Abbott committed various prison minor prison infractions of prison rules to assure they would be locked in the cell all day Sunday.

It was then the men prepared the dummy which they completed even to the hair which Sabin had asked the prison barbers to clip from his head "because of dandruff."

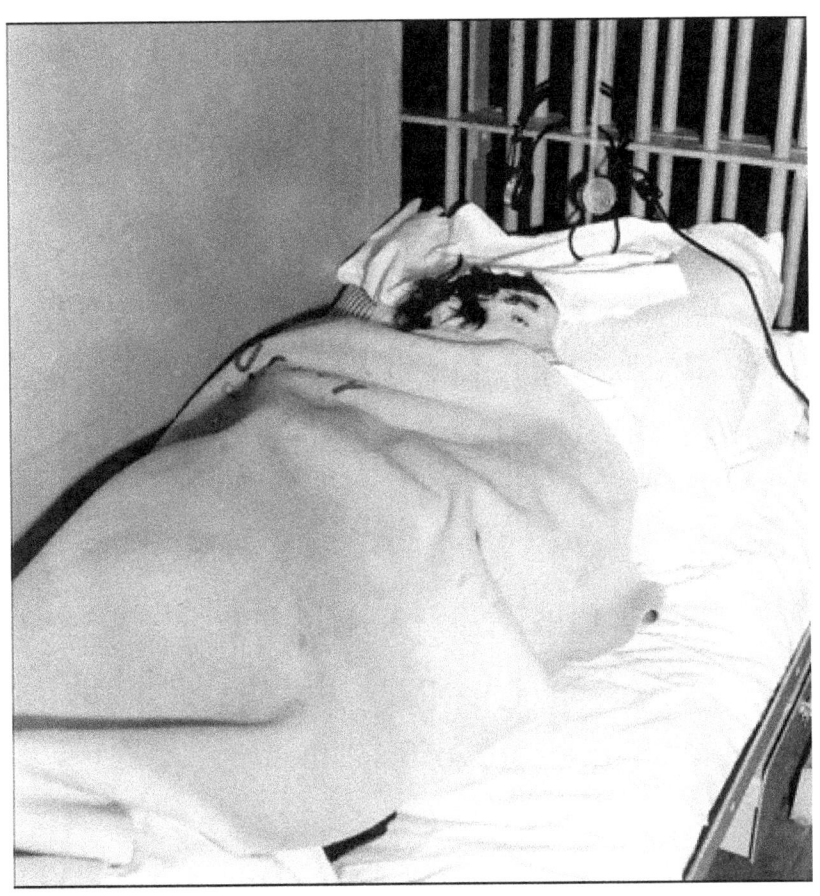

"The Dummy"

HIDES OUT ALL NIGHT.

Abbott apparently hid out Wednesday night, escaped over the wall with a rope made of bed ticking, stole a car belonging to a Folsom resident and headed for Sacramento. The automobile was abandoned a few miles from town when it ran out of gasoline.

Shamblin, the other cell mate, although knowing nothing of the escape. Apparently played no part in helping Abbott, prison officials believe.

L.A.TIMES TEXT:

Braving bullets from the pistols of his jail guards, Dwight E. Abbott, 23 year old life prisoner at Folsom Penitentiary, who came to Los Angeles to "take the rap" for two accused robbers, leaped over a stairway railing in the old Courthouse yesterday and raced through three county buildings before he jumped from a second-story window almost into the arm of a citizen who was attracted to the chase by four deputy sheriffs waving their weapons as they ran.

Stunned by landing on a cement sidewalk, Abbott could make no resistance to his captor, P.M. Reidy, 4062 Ingraham Street, and in the jail hospital later Dr. Benjamin Blank, county physician, said the convict may have a broken back.

As Abbott was standing in the hallway just after recess had been ordered by Superior Judge Willis, presiding at the trial at which the prisoner had just testified, Deputy Sheriff West ordered him to stick out his hands to be handcuffed. It is contrary to law to take a man into court shackled.

Instead of extending his hands, Abbott placed them on a railing, and vaulted to the iron floor of the stairway landing ten feet below. Deputy Sheriffs West and Roberts drew their revolvers, but a crowd of women jurors was standing on the stairway, and the officers could not take the risk of shooting. Bailiff Author Shivell, in Judge Willis's court, who brought back a sharpshooter's medal from overseas twelve years ago, drew a bead on the fleeing convict, but an excited woman blundering into the field of fire probably saved Abbott's life.

The prisoner ran down the front steps of the courthouse and turned south toward the Hall of Records. Bailiff Luskin from Department 18 meanwhile had drawn his pistol and with several bystanders joined the chase.

One of the bystanders who took up the pursuit was Reidy, a real estate salesman, who ran through the Hall of Records and east down an alley to New High Street. Meanwhile the deputies were pursuing their quarry across a bridge from the Hall of Records into an annex where offices of the County Planning Commission are located. Reidy saw the fugitive raise a window and hang from the sill. The man released his hold and dropped Twenty-five feet to the pavement, and stunned by the fall, seemed unable to rise. Reidy pounced on him and held him until Bailiffs Luskin and Shivell ran up with their handcuffs.

In the courtroom after the chase, Abbott excused by Judge Willis and ordered back to the penitentiary, protested that he was in great pain and could not walk over to the jail.

"If you could run that fast, you can certainly walk", said Deputy Sheriff West, jerking the prisoner to his feet and hauling him across to the jail.

In the jail hospital, Abbott was examined by Dr. Blank, who said an X-ray would be necessary to determine whether the prisoner's back or legs are broken.

After recess Judge Willis admonished the jury not to permit the knowledge of Abbott's attempt to escape to influence their deliberations in the case of Charles Lee Quinn and Roy Vernon Quinn whose second trial for the robbery of the Lotus Café in Pasadena is nearing its close.

Abbott had been brought from Folsom by Attorney C. J. Orbison, for the defense and testified that he and not the Quinn brothers, held up the café May 26, 1930, and robbed Robert Mullins, the proprietor, of $130.

Although witnesses in the café identified the Quinns, four police officers from the Lincoln Heights Jail testified that Roy Quinn was a prisoner at the time of the robbery. Deputy District Attorney, Paiton, prosecuting argued that Roy, being a trustee, might have left the jail long enough to commit the robbery.

Abbott was in the County Jail awaiting trial for robbery, when he met the Quinn boys and there, they say, confessed to the crime of which they were accused. Later Abbott was brought back from Folsom where he subsequently had been sentenced to a life term, as a habitual criminal and testified at the first trial of the Quinns. A conviction had at this trial was reversed and a new trial ordered. Attorneys probably will conclude argument at today's session of the trial and the case will go to the jury.

THE SECOND ARTICLE IS FOUND IN THE RENO NEVADA GAZETTE JUNE 16, 1932. IT READS:

Felon Escapes From California Prison

FOLSOM PRISON, Calif., June 16,-(UP)- Dwight E. Abbott, 24, Los Angeles robber, escaped from Folsom prison last night and his absence was not discovered until the general lock-up late today, prison officials said.

Warden Court Smith discovered Abbott had made a dummy with a plaster of paris face, adorned with real hair cut from the heads of him and his cellmate. The dummy, seen in his bed, was lifelike enough to deceive guards.

Skippy and I;
often 'wonder';
Were the Following pictures;
actually:

WITNESS

PROTECTION

?

Dwight Elsworth Abbott CCC
(affectionately: " wight")

Dwight Abbott (wight): "I handle 'em' with gloves for they are growing now and chew my fingers all up"

A 'RECALLED' BIOGRAPHY OF DWIGHT ELSWORTH SR.

-known by his peers as "Rattles Wight"

Dear Fam.,

Our memories of many of our dad's "clues" are fading. Many times he talked in "riddles" tainted with humor. We have put together some conversations and "stories" that; at the time, we thought were just "embellished" fantasies. However; the look in his eyes, as he told these stories, always seemed, somehow, much deeper than second hand recall. We can recall the twinkle in his eyes lighting up like a "stage", fully populated with real characters. It appears that the truth is almost unbelievable; AND much 'stranger than fiction'.

In an abbreviated recap; dad, an abandoned child and pre-teen runaway, became involved in a Los Angeles branch of a Chicago Gang called "The Outfit." It was in its infancy in L.A. during prohibition. Its activities included Money laundering, extortion, prostitution, bootlegging etc. The Outfit was not necessarily part of the Italian Mafia; but, both were "united" as members of a "union of crime bosses" called the "Commission". At times, they all got along, and at other times, they were at odds? Dad referred to the "Commission" in many of his stories.

It appears that Dad, being "underage"; with a built-in sympathetic history & background of child abandonment and abuse, was taking the "Rap" for crimes he either did or did not do.

He was being paid by the Outfit to do this in order to take the "heat" off of the real culprits, who were hardened, repeat criminals subject to much "stiffer" sentences; including hanging. The police were also paid by bagmen to "finger" dad as the "crook". Witnesses were paid to recall dads features and presence. Dad was well known and actually on friendly terms with the LA police. "His" rap sheet contained many convictions for crimes he may or may not have committed; but yet confessed to. He was on more than one life term.

When dad made his "staged" break, from Folsom, via the staircase in the Old L.A. Courthouse on may 7, 1931; deputies: West, Roberts and Shivell were all part of the act. They had been very well paid. They made up stories why they couldn't "shoot" . If the real estate agent had not grabbed dad; while dad was lying stunned on the sidewalk, dad would have made the "amazing escape."

It appears that the one news article above; involved a "double cross" ; of dads then ,"boss"; a guy named "Dizzy Joe". Dizzy had given his word that dad would be released (as usual) after taking the Rap for these crooks. It turns out that these "crooks" were actually originally hired by a guy named "Dragon Jack" to rub out Dizzy Joe. Dad somehow got word that arrangements to "escape" had been made; but, dad did not make it, as you can see. Neither did Dizzy; appears he was rubbed out within days of dad going back to prison.

At this point Dad "appealed" to the head of the Outfit; a guy called "Scarface". It turns out Scarface, (who apparently was Al Capone) felt dad had proven himself "loyal"; even though Capone backed Dragon Jack. Subsequently orders were given through a guy named "Bottles" down to a guy named "Greasy". Greasy was the "bagman arranger'. The bagman transfers the cash.

Dad used to take us to a little restaurant near east L.A. He called it "Joe's Greasy Spoon"? Whenever we went, Dad would ask, if "Greasy" was around? This fairly rotund guy would come out and say, with a thick Italian accent: "Hey, Rattles, how's you family?!" He would always ask Skippy, with a very serious, concerned air, if he needed more cheese in my grilled cheese sandwich. He would always reply that it was, already, too much. Greasy would then say that we "were his best customer; saving him money and keeping him in business!" Might have this been the selfsame "Greasy", who had taken orders from "Bottles?"

This bagman paid off a councilman/mayor named Shaw. Shaw made a "deal" for a "new" trial through the district attorney/prosecutor who arranged for the trial to have a "well paid" judge, who was also a member of the "Commission".

Dad was retried on a charge of aiding and abetting racketeering and extortion. He was given 3 years' probation, for "good behavior" and being a minor, when many of "his" worst crimes were committed. He also was "given" a paid administrative job of community service in the California Conservation Corps (CCC).

Somehow many trial records and convictions were "misplaced" and/or destroyed in a fire and his "record" was wiped clean.

Fortunately, about this time, Al Capone, Dads next scheduled boss, was jailed for tax evasion. Dad was somewhat "indentured", at this point and was "farmed out" for the time being. Due to dad's dual police and criminal contacts, dad was assigned as a "street wise host" for a Chicago newcomer, who was "transferred" to the west coast operations. The newcomer liked dad right away.

Dad was quickly promoted to be an emissary and courier. Dad made many trips back and forth from El Monte and Beverly Hills, California, to Las Vegas, Nevada, and back. The newcomer, at one time, told dad; that; they might be 'related'?

The newcomer was Benjamin (Bugsy) Siegel. Siegel was involved in constructing the Flamingo Hotel, which he eventually took over, even though he did not like Nevada. We remember exploring, in the desert, behind the Flamingo on many of dads trips. Dad also spent a lot of time at the "Silver Slipper" across from the Flamingo. During this time, Siegel also made it a point to hob-nob with the Hollywood crowd, as the studios were a target of the Commission.

He frequently represented Dad, as "his boy."

As unlikely, as it may sound, dad was among the few underlings that actually was convicted, given life sentences; incarcerated, released to freedom and never went back.

Dad told us, one time, that he owed any "success" in who, what; and where he was today, to keeping his mouth shut and NOT asking ANY questions!. The look in his eyes and his tone of voice has kept our mouths shut until this day!

It was during this time that Dad was introduced to our Grandmother, Marguerite Stevens - Rubendale- Hemstreet. Grandma was Doris Difraso's cook. Difraso was one of Siegel's Hollywood girlfriends and informant.

An intriguing and amazing love story followed, which involved our Grandmother's daughter, Betty (Stevens) Abbott; our mother.

It comes with many twists - Stay Tuned....

There is quite a bit we left out, as we are still in awe of how our memories are coming together.

And, if you find this hard to believe, you might find the "follow-up" even harder……. we say this, as memories of particular incidents begin to return: for example, who was the "Mystery Man" our dad called "Uncle Charlie"?

We actually thought he was our only living relative, on my dad's side. He occasionally came from "somewhere" very far away to "visit". He spent short periods of time with dad, mom, Skippy and Sonny. Yet, his "nickname" and/or that of his son was; also: "Sonny"? Why did he carry several bullet casings and spent slugs in his pockets? Why was one slug, in particular, so meaningful to him…? It was framed in an engraved "good luck" medallion.

Sitting on our small cement back-porch one day;
he reached into his pocket pulling out what
appeared to us, as a massive handful of change and
asked each of us, to choose whatever we wanted. I
noticed the bullet medallion under the change and
reached for it. I saw his eyes well up with tears, as I
grasped the medallion. I quickly let it go and took a
sitting liberty quarter. Not much later, that
medallion was given to me by my dad. He looked at
me, with his eyes very damp and full of hurt, and

said: "Uncle Charlie" would not be back, and Charlie wanted me to have the medallion.

How was dad able to get us out of "petty crimes" we committed? Why did our dad, using a large caterpillar tractor; periodically, bury cars under 30 feet of dirt, in a large natural hidden gully on our property?

Skippy came home from school, one day, and saw a lot of dozer work in the gully. He asked what happened. Dad said he had to bury his car! And sure enough His car was gone!? Skippy knew better than to ask any more questions.

How and why did we come by a custom made gaming table with switches and levers that could transform itself into a normal coffee table in a matter of seconds? My dad hosted parties deep into the night with people I did not know. How did my half-brother, David, really get shot a couple of weeks before dad buried the car?. Why did we move soon after the shooting and car burial?

We went back to El Monte, and 'bought' a home next door to a very friendly Italian family, who just happened to be former friends of Dad and mom? Why did this family, simply, vanish one day; after about six months?

Who was "Snow-baby", "Angel" , "Denmark", "Nette" ," "Mac-body", "Shorty" and "Snorky", etc. Why did most every friend of my dads have a "nick-name" and not a "real name?" How was dad able to help my brother, Sonny, for so long; yet eventually fail? Did his old "contacts" eventually disappear? Who did we actually meet in Florida, when we flew there to visit dads "relatives". We were told they were our "cousins….?"

Did dad really enter the Army and how come we have service records in two different branches of the service with two commissions….? Why did I follow in my dad's footsteps and Skippy did not…? The questions go on…….the answers are there;

however, as with my brother; we may not want to really know. Forced ignorance may be our; and our families, most expedient option.

As Memory serves,

Written in Love, by Dwight Abbott and Danny Abbott; [Sonny & Skippy] in memory of Dad; Dwight Elsworth Abbott

BEAR MOUNTAIN;

Silverthorn California
"Brother Bear"

After years of incarceration, once I was released from prison; it became my choice to wander homeless throughout beautiful Shasta County with my girlfriend, Mary Ann Rice, and my dog Sate, a loyal and protective Doberman Pincher. Living in my van, free to come and go, not a bother to anyone other than a cop who decided he didn't like the fact that the registration tag on my license plate had expired.

One unlucky day he pulled me over and I was arrested for "outstanding traffic warrants." Mary Ann took Sate (short for 'Satan') and the van was towed. I would never see it again.

After serving a 90 day jail sentence, 45 days half time, I went in search of Mary Ann; only to find she had a new boyfriend; a really nice guy, who offered her a home; I never would be able to, unless I returned to armed robberies, which I was trying not to do.

She had thought to grab our large tent from the van, which I gratefully accepted, along with Sate. As I exited her boyfriend's car and disappeared into the Silverthorn Hidden Valley Wilderness, as with the van, I knew I'd not see Mary Ann again.

My nearly yearlong stay, hidden atop a thickly forested mountain, would be the most exhilarating experience of my life. Inexplicably the accepting creatures there, would invite me to become one with them and the mountain.

Campsite on Bear Mountain
above and South of Silverthorn Resort
North and above Hidden Valley Market

My first nights, I was frightened, if that is the right word describing what I felt. I knew I was being watched. Beyond my small campfire, the shimmery glow of many eyes peering at me from the thick bushes and trees kept me awake, while Sate purred a deep, throaty growl.

As the nights passed I began to realize not all of these creatures remained camouflaged by the darkness, appearing instead to find the illuminating fire inviting and not their enemy.

Both sides, seeming to realize neither meant harm to the other, Sate had given up sounding the alarm. I did not know it then, but we were fast becoming one upon the mountain.

First there was "Old Raccoon", then "Scrawny Wolf"; both obviously quite hungry, seemingly willing to risk whatever life was left them to beg a morsel. Though at first I had little, I shared. Only the most heartless would have done less. Each day, watching one another closely, they moved closer to savor the tidbits, as though any could be their last, and might well have been, considering the shape they appeared to be in. It was quite obvious their hunting and foraging days were numbered, if not over, had it not been for my arrival.

One cold morning I awakened to find toothless Old Raccoon sleeping at my feet inside the tent. Scrawny Wolf took to sleeping between the tent and the glowing embers of the dying fire. In the gloom he resembled a log, but Sate's posture told me he knew it was not so. The nights I looked out to find Scrawny was not there, I would fret. It was pure relief I felt when I would see him staring at me in the morning.

Months into my wanna-be 'mountain man' existence, I was casually folding back a flap of the tent entrance when the thought came to me: "Where are the critters that had taken to waiting outside for the food I would throw?" I leaned forward, glanced to my left, and froze. Sitting no further than two to three yards from the tent was a reasonably large bear! He? she?, casually turned it's big head toward me. Silently we stared at one another. I would have wrenched back had I not known Old Raccoon was at my feet, as he was each morning, shaking off his night's sleep with a wide yawn.

Though I had never been able to shoot an animal, I glanced up to take comfort that one of my rifles was secured directly above the tent's entry. Then the stench reached me.

After a few nights and days of his continued presence, it became obvious "Brother Bear" had adopted us. As I moved around outside, it also was obvious Sate and I were welcome on his mountain. "Mi Case su Casa!"

I never felt it a prudent move to check if Brother Bear was a male or female. It was obvious he was quite old. His fur caked with dirt, pebbles and twigs. He had a constant itch, always on his right haunch. Hard as he tried, he couldn't reach it. Rubbing it on surrounding brush, to satisfy it, didn't work.

Came a time Brother Bears odor no longer offended my senses. I took to sitting beside him, close as I dared. He seemed to ignore me, but I knew better. Using my left hand, I cautiously reached over to gently scratch his haunch. I felt him stiffen slightly, and after relax. Scared the hell out of me. His fur was stiff, coarse, unlike Sate's, who lay some distance away intently watching. I knew he had to be thinking I was crazy.

My fingers found the sore I thought was the source of his bother. Brother Bear appeared almost human when he looked over at me, in his eyes; a 'thank you'. Each night following, Brother Bear would sit near me, obviously expecting his nightly cleaning and massage. There were a number of times I felt I could stop only after he began to doze.

As I had for several months, I awakened one morning expecting Old Raccoon to waddle out from 'our' sleeping bag, where he had taken to burrowing. When he didn't move from my leg, where he snuggled through each night, nor make that strange clicking sound, I reached down to find the little fella had passed sometime during the chilly night. I felt tears well; I cried.

Somehow sensing the others would want to be there, I waited until late evening to bury our friend. As I pushed dirt into the grave, Brother Bear, Scrawny Wolf and Sate lay nearby, while others watched from the trees and bushes. I wondered if Old Raccoon knew how many friends he was leaving behind?

For days, nights and weeks after, I enjoyed a menagerie of critters that learned there was no need to fear me; nor, I them. There was in the trees; I never knew it to leave; a cougar. I saw it only once on the ground. Every night I knew it was close by the oddly gentle sound as it snored. I am sure Sate kept an eye on it, as did I.

One morning I noticed a change in the typically cool air; it was becoming downright cold. My friends had stopped visiting the camp. I'd heard gunfire in the far distance before this change in the weather, and could but hope none of the little guys had met up with the hunters.

Soon after a particularly bitter cold set in I awakened to a foot of snow and watched flakes appearing as large as 'softballs' fall. Ignorant city boy I was, instinct kicked in late. I knew Sate and I were in serious trouble. Silverthorn Resort was about two and one half miles from the camp....'If I could reach it'. That was a huge 'if''.

Wasting no time from then, I grabbed one of my rifles, a box of shells and dressed warmly, as I had been prepared for the cold days and nights. With Sate leading the way, we began our journey through the ever deepening snow. There is little to no doubt we would not have made it save for the fact we knew well the now snow covered concealed path.

The "Path" ending about 50 yards North of Silverthorn Resort Store and Restaurant; January 8, 2016

Trusting my faithful companion, I followed him.

Thigh deep in dry snow, every step pulling at our legs, we grew exhausted. Holding on to Sate, I pushed while he pulled. No matter the heavy clothes I had on, my extremities began to numb. I worried about this. There was no doubt my friend knew the fix we were in. In my mind I began to go over how best to carry him; should that time come. I could not have imagined leaving him, no more than he would have left me.

More than a couple feet in front of us I could see nothing. Then, without warning, the snow gave way and Sate tumbled down to come to a halt under a roof's overhang. There I fell atop him. We both lay for a moment, catching our breath, while I stared at a door.

Silverthorn Resort "Overhang and Door"
January 8, 2016

It had taken somewhere near three hours, more likely closer to four, to travel a bit less than two miles on a reasonably straight path, once we had reached the base of the mountain where we had our camp.

I discovered not a soul had remained at the resort. Even the burly "Security Guard" I had become acquainted with, who knew we were living on the mountain, was gone. The heavy doors locked, in desperation I broke a window, pushed Sate through, and found myself in the foyer leading to a reception hall. There the quiet was 'eerie'. Sate continued to pant heavily as we went into the large hall.

Leaving the foyer I discovered to my immediate left a small, open-front boutique. To my right was a small delicatessen and grocery store from which, I quickly noted, all perishable foods had been removed. Obviously the resort's staff had anticipated the worst. I began to suspect it was like this every year.

Gas and electricity had been shut off. For hours I searched for a circuit box, in vain. I did find a welcome cache of canned foods, some of which I excitedly opened with my hunting knife. A few cans of fruit I stuffed into my backpack.

Whenever I think of this time I cannot but wonder where the hell that box was?

Lost "circuit box" found on January 8, 2016 - Outside the Window I broke.

I did discover a large generator, for which I was unable to locate fuel. 'What is an emergency generator good for without fuel?' Obviously it had to be somewhere! I never found it.

Silverthorn Resort "Fuel Supply" was Found,
on January 8, 2016;
across the street where I broke the window
and entered.

Fortunately there was some nice sailing and hiking gear still hanging on the racks. From the price tags I gathered the clothing was not meant for folks like me: more for those who moored their multi-million dollar boats down at the dock during the summer months.

The only way I would ever wear such finery is by doing what I was about to do, steal it!

I quickly stripped off my half frozen garments and shivered my way into a yellow outfit and black boots that nearly fit me. I even found a doggie sweater, $168.00, and leather booties, $87.00. Yikes!

After a day and night of rest, with a clear head, I tried to figure a way out of the mess Sate and I were in. It all came back to understanding my choices were limited: Remain, or chance another nearly six miles off the mountain. In desperation, I spent several more hours looking for gasoline and the circuit box before making my choice. The next morning Sate and I began what would be a merciless journey.

There is no doubt, had I not been physically and mentally in my prime, I would have been foolish and chosen to remain at the resort, where come spring, the snows melted, it is most likely Sate and I, our bodies frozen, would have been found.

We began making our way on a road that had had one last snowplow scraped over it, I assumed, as everyone left. Soon in waist-high snow, we struggled from early dawn to late dusk. Just as it began to again snow heavily we reached the base of the mountain. Sate became excited. He had spotted the small "Hidden Valley Market", country store we had visited several times the past year; after I realized it was not in me to take the lives of the animals on the mountain, no matter how hungry I became. I'd rather walk the many miles down to purchase the foods Sate and I needed time to time.

Hidden Valley Market with Upstair 'Cabin'.

There was a private residence just above the store. From a chimney along the side, smoke drifted lazily into the sky.

Hidden Valley Market's Chimney from the outside

Inviting us to hurry, were windows with a golden glow peeking out from behind the shut curtains.

I knocked at the door, after which an elderly man cautiously looked out a window. Uninvited guests at that time of year had to be viewed with considerable suspicion. While he looked me up and down, I was glad Sate and I looked good in our fancy clothes. His wife led us before a huge rock fireplace where we were allowed to warm ourselves.

The "Fireplace";
inside Hidden Valley Market;
found on January 8, 2016;
long ago ordered sealed by the fire marshal.
Yet; it's warmth still felt,, as fisherfolk share
tall tales!

The snow on my jacket and boots melted, on the floor the puddles quickly dried. About that time the woman recognized Sate, and then me, after a closer look. I could see her relax.

I accepted hot stew. The memory of that evening makes my mouth water, as I write. A small, rather cute, dog, enamored at Sate's stature, shared what was in her bowl. I was asked many questions, after which the gentleman drove us down to civilization. Redding, California had never looked so good. To those folks I have always been grateful. It had been a close call, one of the most amazing in my lifetime.

Other than the clothes I left inside the resort, and the rifle I packed out with me, everything I owned was left on the mountain. After the snows melted, could be Old Raccoon's wood cross near the abandoned tent, pistols, rifles and what little else I possessed was discovered, bringing to life a number of questions. Before the storm hit there had been a couple of people nosing around within a mile or so of my camp. It was beginning to get crowded up that way.

This story has reminded me of the afternoon when the Judge sentenced me to four consecutive life sentences. In a quite courtroom, the Judge shared, "You are an animal, Mr. Abbott!" I chose to ignore his observation. In chains, short-stepping because of the heavy leg irons, I left the courtroom. As I stepped into the anteroom, from the crowd dawdling there, a female voice shouted, "Are you an animal, like the judge said, Mr. Abbott?"

I do not know if I spoke aloud, or if I whispered, or if it was no more than a thought: "I am much worse, lady. I am human!"

Recently a teenage boy read this story at my website, DwightAbbott.com. He became excited upon finding such a world existed, something other than the troubled life his problems were handing him. He wrote that after telling his grandmother about my story she told him "Brother Bear" could not be true, that what I wrote is ...."only a story."

I wrote back to share with him that though she means well, **everything**, all my works, are non-fiction; and Brother Bear was most certainly real, as was Old Raccoon and Scrawny Wolf: creatures who invited me into their world, believing they could trust me, believing I meant them no harm.

I wished the child the best in this hard life, and hoped he would find his mountain some day.

CONVICT AND THE GOPHER:

A Tale of Trust

Convict and the Gopher
A Tale of Trust

Fact is, if you feed a starving animal it is
unlikely he will bite you. That, dear family, is
the principle difference between them and man.
Once I was told I am an animal; yet always
I've known I am much worse – I am human.

R. I. P. POPCORN

If you feed a starving animal, it is unlikely he will bit you.
That, dear Family, is the principle difference between them and man.
Once I was told I am an "animal",
yet always I've known I am much worse - I am human

Dwight Abbott

February 2007 - Popcorn was the runt of what was undoubtedly a recent litter; a tiny creature having the misfortune of being forced from his home somewhere underground. He was discovered wandering the prison yard, meandering at the feet of grizzled and long-hardened prisoners, left with no choice but to be out among those that every fiber of his being screamed out to him not to trust - the long-proven most dangerous of all in the animal kingdom calling themselves 'human'.

I must have appeared at least a hundred feet tall before I bent my old knees to hunker down and hold out my hand to what I thought was an injured mouse. To my surprise, the obviously frightened creature crawled, possibly in desperation, onto my hand where he immediately collapsed, exhausted from his ordeal.

Not wanting to frighten him any more than he already was; slowly I raised my hand to where I could see him clearly. There I discovered, not a mouse, but a very tiny gopher, holding in his teeth a kernel of popped corn he'd discovered somewhere along his way. I suspected he was no more than two-three weeks old, his pink skin peeking through sparse fur yet to fill in. I looked into black eyes staring suspiciously back at me. What was he thinking? Could it have been, "I'm so tired and scared: Should I run? Should I stay? Where would I go, if I got away? Nobody wants me."

Through many years here I'd seen hundreds of these little guys scampering across the dirt, leading me to believe their mothers banish them from the nest, while they are still very young. This one, I held, was scratched and bleeding, obviously much too young to be out on its own as it was; its fate subject to chance.

Imagine, if you can, being scooped up by a giant. Quite scary; I am certain it would be. Yet, though obviously suspicious; on my hand, sat quietly this courageous gopher, sharing with me a "a moment", while I wondered, if he was going to bite me. Certainly he had to be asking himself what I intended; and, if he would need to defend himself against this human.

Then I saddened. Could it be the reason he had not run was he'd decided to accept what he believed was to be his fate as so many before him; aunts, uncles, brothers and sisters, caught by the most cruel of all? "What are my chances that I will enjoy another early morn's dawn, frolic about, and dig tunnels - my most favorite past time? I know, in your eyes, I'm just a bothersome rodent, though kinda cute you got to admit.... Could there be hope for me?" We stared.

Carefully, I lowered him to the ground from which I had lifted him moments before, returning to him his precious freedom. Knowing as I do what it feels like to have liberty denied, the thought to take his never entered my mind.

"This is not a nice place, partner. Go on, get out of here." He didn't budge. I gave him a gentle poke on his butt. That didn't work for him. "What you going to do, little fella?" I had expected him to instantly dash off to be the gopher he was born to be; yet, there he sat, unmoving. Was it his innate curiosity, native to all who forage; stilling him, or was he weighting what his odds were of getting away?

While he considered his options, I remained squatting; the back of my open hand pressed against the ground. This gopher had to be on its way, and I'd decided to watch out for him, make sure he remained safe until I was ordered back to my burrow: a hot, humid, concrete box I have existed in for more than 50 years. Once there, I'd will myself to quickly forget this creature that, from seemingly from nowhere, had come into my weary existence; somehow managing to touch me where I had not been touched for a very long time - 'feeling' being an often far too expensive luxury here in my world.

No doubt a long and trying day of self-preservation, he proceeded to stretch, his tiny paws, reaching; appearing to invite me again to pick him up. Then, to my astonishment, he crawled back onto the palm of my hand, there to immediately curl into a furry ball and go to sleep. He had made his choice, and I was about to make mine.

I peered around, making sure none of the near guards were watching me. There are those who would take this hapless animal from me and do terrible things. Others would admire, though often grudging, the trust that had begun between this unlikely pair in the middle of a maximum security prison yard. The latter would, in all probability, choose to say nothing about the 'rules' dictating that inmates are not allowed to have pets.

Furtively, I slipped "Popcorn" into my shirt's breast pocket. Should he awaken, I hoped he'd somehow sense he had to remain perfectly still.

"Yard is closed! Report back to your cell blocks," came the anticipated announcement over the intercom speakers strewn throughout the institution. I asked my partner to distract whichever guard stood ready to search us, so I could sneak Popcorn, through and into our cell. Fortunately it was a Correctional Officer we both knew would elect not to draw attention to our gopher should he discover it, while running his hands over my body looking for miniscule "contraband items" such as knives, machine guns and atomic bombs.

As luck would have it, when I presented myself for this daily humiliation; so did my new buddy, poking his head up over the hem of my pocket. The guard looked at him staring fearlessly back, smiled and instructed, "Take good care of that little guy, you hear?"

"Don't need to worry about him," I responded in a conspiratorial tone.

Back at our "house," my cell partner, Raymond, and I discussed how we would make our new cell mate comfortable. Could a gopher, this creature born in dirt, naturally living its entire life digging through it, be made at home in our difficult circumstances; confinement inside a concrete cage?

"What about food? How will we feed him, Raymond? Don't they live by eating roots, stuff like that"; in ignorance; I questioned?

In ignorance, Raymond looked at me, confusion clouding his face.

How do I know, Sonny? I ain't no hamster!"

"He's no hamster, Ray, he's a gopher."

"What's the difference?"

I surrendered. "Forget it! We got to do something; he won't leave."

"I guess we'll have to figure it out," my cellie answered.

"Duh!" Back to square one.

We paid five coveted First Class U.S. Postage Stamps for a cardboard apple-packing box, handed off to us, as we returned from our evening shower. Only after padding it with towels and adding a plastic lid removed from a Folgers' Instant Coffee jar that Ray filled with water, did I lift soundly sleeping Popcorn from my pocket. Inside the box he looked up at me, seeming to ask if everything was okay.

Satisfied it was, he burrowed into his waiting 'blankets,' returning to his slumber from which I had so rudely awakened him.

In the Chow Line, Raymond thought to remove from his food tray - "for the hamster" - pieces of lettuce, two string beans and the corner from a piece of stale bread; all, I placed beside the lid before carefully pushing the box under my bunk.

Through the night, as any new father would, I checked on Popcorn. It was not until late morning he peeked out from under the towels. After taking a careful look around, he waddled over to investigate our offerings left the night before. He first grabbed up a small piece of lettuce to nibble until it was gone. Next, a string bean quickly disappeared before he scooped the rest into his mouth until his cheek pouches were bulging. He would not go hungry later.

"Maybe he's a chipmunk," Ray dryly observed. I

ignored him, at the same time noticing Popcorn had ignored his water dish. "Don't surprise me none; guards won't drink it either," I muttered. It would be a couple of days before I understood gophers do not 'drink'. They instead hydrate themselves through the foods they eat.

Quite mysteriously, tiny dark pellets appeared from under towels that had begun to pitch about; drawing my attention. Popcorn was kicking them out from his 'nest' before scampering out to a far corner of the box; turn to back in, and wee-wee before again returning to his dig. He would teach me: gophers choose not to pee anywhere near where they lie. They are remarkably clean and tidy animals; a revelation I am sure will surprise people, considering these creatures live their entire lives, as I have already written, burrowed in dirt.

One day while tinkering around; using a razor blade, I cut in half a Saltine Cracker box and fashioned a small room in *that* corner. The next morning I discovered Popcorn had, through the night, faithfully visited his 'private bathroom'.

Unfortunately gophers can, by their very nature, be destructive. However, it's not something they do because they are ornery; they are not. They need to constantly chew, even when sleeping, to grind their teeth together - all four of them - to keep their top two from growing down into their lower jaw. Popcorn began immediately to take apart the towels I'd given him, causing me to worry a guard would note "state property" was being "deliberately destroyed," in turn search through our cell for more, discover Popcorn and likely take him from us.

To avoid this, I exchanged his "blankets" with several of my personal cotton undergarments, and additionally gave him one of my Sketcher's tennis shoes to gnaw on (sorry Skippy), which he thoroughly enjoyed for years.

I doubt 'reason' will trump here in any argument I might encounter, convinced, as I am, that Popcorn knew what was okay to chew; what not. Whatever was under the bunk was his. All else, set on the floor, was not to be molested. His 'understanding' of this was made obvious when he first thought I was not paying him attention. He grabbed hold of a 'tasty looking morsel,' and began to drag it under the bunk where he could have his way with it. First there was a sock, my slipper, a pair of Levi pants, several rolls of toilet paper, a sponge I have paid another prison three postage stamps for....

Two, possibly three, days after Popcorn adopted us, while typing my manuscript, CONSEQUENCE: the aftermath, and eating morning porridge, there came an urgent scratching on one of my toes. I reached down and Popcorn leaped to grab hold of my sweatshirt, disappearing immediately into the right sleeve. This began a daily ritual enjoyed between us lasting more than four years - Popcorn always going for the right sleeve, having an aversion to the left.

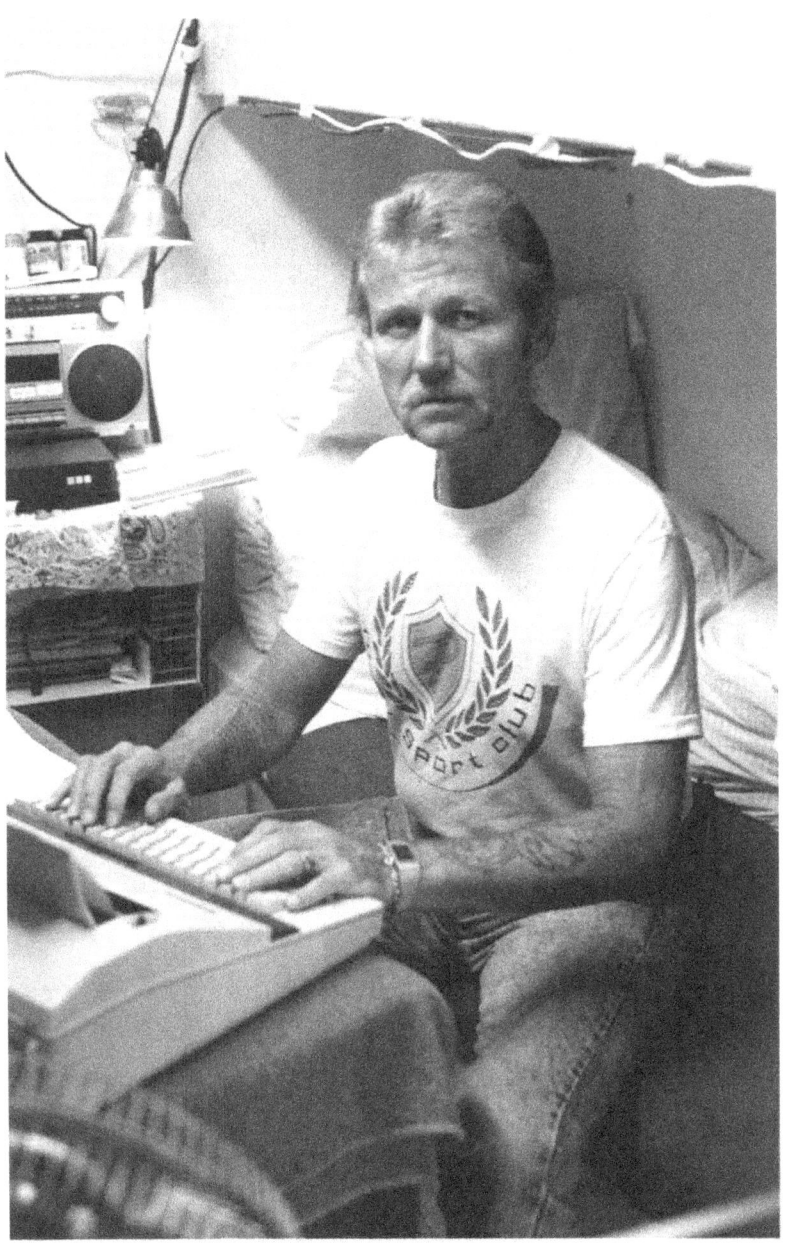

Turning back to my typewriter, with no thought Popcorn had decided there would be changes made to my routine, I saw him peeking out from the shirt's cuff, his tiny nose sniffing about. First making sure the porridge was not hot, using the tip of my plastic spoon, I offered him a portion of my oatmeal.

Each morning after, his wet nose barely poking out from his preferred place of concealment - under the hem of my right sleeve - he'd patiently wait. Like father; like son; Popcorn's favorite flavored instant oatmeal, was "Maple and Brown Sugar", purchased at the inmate Canteen, where, unfortunately, my prison trust account causes me financial embarrassment. Grudging Popcorn not; this did add to an already long list of "deals to be made." It was fortunate; I play Texas Hold 'Em better than most around here, who seem convinced they are Kenny Rogers.

I'm not sure, when it was, Popcorn began to deposit items he foraged throughout the cell into his food dish; nor when I discovered that, if I were to remove from it, something he put there; and place it elsewhere, he'd sense his 'stuff' had been messed with and immediately come out to investigate from wherever he had burrowed. Without fail, he'd retrieve the item and return it to the exact spot in his bowl he had originally arranged it.

It was like a doorbell: whenever I wanted to check on

him, make sure he was okay, or just give him some lovin', I would move something he had meticulously set aside.

Sometime during his first nights with us, Popcorn tunneled out of the cardboard box. I awakened the following morning to find him curled into his fur ball, sleeping soundly while snuggled against my neck.

"How'd you get up here, you little escape artist?"

It was a question to be answered days later, when from the corner of my eye I caught movement. Popcorn had leaped up, grabbed onto the blanket, hanging down inches above the floor, from my bunk, and began to climb precariously up to his reward, roaming at will; the vastness of my 3x7 foot bed.

A remarkable feat; considering it was a 90 degree grade; up two feet of fickle blanket, journeyed by a two-ounce creature, whose nature it was to go down; not up.

Through the years to follow, he'd do this until he became frail. One early afternoon I watched him near the top, only to fall backward onto unforgiving concrete. Tough little guy always he was, he righted himself, shook it off, tried again, again and again; before coming to the realization: he no longer had the strength; his climbing days were over. I clearly remember my own mood taking a nose dive, as he tried over and over; myself understanding those activities most enjoyed by him was to be no more. Raymond began laying out a blanket to protect Popcorn from the concrete, "just in case." He, from that time, did no more than look up and pine for 'the day.'

Truth be known; Popcorn had taken command of the cell; each night, and eventually through all the days,. Each evening before retiring to my bunk, I would hide pieces of food he'd later forage throughout the night. In turn I expected to awaken each morning and discover 'treasures' hiding in my socks, shoes, laundry bag, wherever, whatever, he could get into, which was pretty much everywhere and everything. He'd scoop into his cheeks food from his bowl to wait patiently until I picked him up. Off he would go, disappearing into my sweatshirt - our sweatshirt - stashing his goodies; I suppose in case he became hungry while exploring there, chewing, constructing observation posts and escape hatches, and not just to exasperate me.

I've no idea how many sweatshirts he and I went through this way, but it never mattered to me. Somehow I managed to have another at the ready; going out and bargaining on the tier for those gently worn, trading desserts or putting to work my typing skills for "jailhouse lawyers", fighting for their freedom.

Each of our days together would begin, when I sat typing; and, felt him nibble on my heel, announcing his majesty had awakened; always a half hour, give or take a minute or two, after I put together my first "Cadillac" - a 16 oz tumbler filled with hot water, in which Instant Folgers Coffee, sugar and Original Coffee-Mate Creamer is stirred.

Then again, possibly our days began, when; teasing, I would ignore him until he turned again to that spot he had become intimately acquainted with, directly above my heel, to bite down on, harder and harder, never breaking the skin, though he could have easily bitten to the bone; until I surrendered and reached for him; knowing as I did he would run back into the darkness, he loved so much, under my bunk; in turn teasing me. Seconds after, he'd dart out towards me, stop - or try to; first sliding a foot or more over worn concrete - before shifting into reverse and returning again to his burrow; backward.

He would do this a number of times before hopping, literally, onto the palm of my waiting hand, finally granting me the pleasure of his highness's company. Here; I had to be careful holding him, as it was uncertain he would remain, allow me to lift him up, or again suddenly shift into reverse. I was intrigued that he was so much quicker moving backward.

When he decided we'd moved on to the next phase of our game, he would begin to gallop forward, forcing me to place one hand before the other, or he would drop from my lap several feet to the floor - a far distance for a gopher. He'd run until he became bored, never tired. Then playfully - I think he was playing - he'd bite at my hand and demand I return him to the floor. There, he entertained himself a short while before I again felt movement at my feet. Popcorn was letting me know he was ready for another go.

When I experienced my third stroke, Popcorn somehow knew I was not, afterward, myself. As I battled to mend, he became less demanding; more gentle in his ways. My left side paralyzed; I could no longer bend and pluck him from the floor as he had come to expect every early morning.

Popcorn began instead to come out each noontime to sit near the chair, always at my right, and patiently wait for Raymond to awaken after his long night reading; to fold my blanket in a way that when he laid it across my lap, it's ends would gently slope to the floor. Thereafter; through the day, whenever he wanted my attention, Popcorn would climb up to lie on my lap where I'd pet him, while he nibbled on my hand; until he slept with one of my fingers still in his mouth.

Often he'd lie dreaming on his back, little legs stretched out; appearing to invite a hug. I would return to what I was not yet convinced to be an impossible assignment: teaching myself how to type 30-40 words a minute using only my right hand while struggling to complete CONSEQUENCE; concerned I would not accomplish either before I died.

I am unable to recall when I first noticed Popcorn's once shiny brown and gold fur had dulled; nor, the gray under his chin and over his stomach that had mysteriously appeared; as the gray in my, once, blond hair. I do clearly remember; it was our fourth Christmas morning together, 2010, when I detected Popcorn was having difficulty climbing up the blanket that Raymond placed on my lap each late morning. It came to me then that I was not the only one growing old, and feeling it.

Way I figured it, the following February 2011 would make it four years since the three of us bunked-up together in this 6x12 foot cage. Didn't seem like a whole lot of time until Raymond reminded me it was 'three lifetimes' for Popcorn; these creatures often living no more than a year, two if they are exceptionally lucky in the wild. My mood became somber: "Could it be Popcorn is not going to be with me much longer?"

Mid-morning, April 27th, I sensed something was wrong. I stopped typing and looked down. There on the floor, beside my wheelchair, Popcorn was turning in circles. I felt my heart do a hiccup and begin beating against the inside of my chest. Something was terribly wrong with him. I cried out; asked Raymond to hand our friend up to me; where, on my lap, he appeared to calm, his left paw finding my finger to grasp as always before; but this time, it felt different to me; desperate.

For several minutes Raymond looked on from where he sat at the edge of my bunk before deciding to 'risk' telling me what he thought was going on. He knew I was in denial, that any mention of 'it' happening made me angry. No way could I accept that Popcorn's journey through this life, most of which he had shared with me, was nearing its end.

Gently, I took him into my right hand, held him up where we stared into one another's eyes. I felt his paws push at my palm as he tried to stand, to begin his day with me as; we had together, so many times before. I noticed his cheeks were, as always, filled with foraged 'treasures' he had intended to take with him into my shirt and secret there. I turned my face away from Ray, hiding tears that had unexpectedly begun to well in my eyes.

"What's wrong, little guy?" I could not doubt; he was trying to figure that out himself. Only moments before,

Popcorn had furtively hastened out from beneath my bunk, leaving behind the darkness from which he had been peering, waiting for the moment I was not giving him attention, when he could run under my chair unnoticed. Then suddenly, but inches from the foot he had been about to munch, he could go no further. He tried and he tried, but his right side refused to cooperate.

What followed were five very long days before Popcorn died, May 2, 2011, at 6:56 a.m., while I held him wrapped in his blanket; the piece, I had years before, torn from my soft cotton T-shirt. I hoped then, and now, he recognized it's feel, and was comforted by it. I was certain, by then, he knew what was going on; just as I had reluctantly accepted that we had but a short time left together.

Seconds before he left me, my lips brushing against his fur, I whispered, "Thank you for the memories" - memories that I've since, selfishly, guiltily, tried to shake from my head; painful as they can be, especially late at night, when comes a sound from under my bunk, I'd swear was cardboard being chewed; or a brief whisper of movement I remember in the midnight silence, when I can't stop pleading for an answer to my question: "Did I do the right thing not returning him to the yard once he was big enough to find off the bullies?" Keeping him had been in contradiction to my lifelong belief wild animals should never be kept.

I awakened Ray as I gently wrapped Popcorn's tiny body with a white shroud; torn from the cloth upon which he died, and lay him inside the casket Raymond had painstakingly constructed days before.

Together, we buried Popcorn out on the prison yard, under which he had been born. Quite unexpectedly, several of our associates, hearing through the prison grapevine that "Sonny and Ray's Gopher died," gathered near us to pay Popcorn their respects; to honor his journey through this life by acknowledging it.

McNeil Island
Penitentiary

As I looked around at their faces, it nearly shoved me over the edge upon which I'd been teetering. I was deeply, deeply touched that this creature, weighing in at no more than maybe four ounces, half of which was a fur ball; both in life and in death; melted hardened hearts of convicts, killers of men, among whom there was not a dry eye; each tried, but failed to hide.

I watched Raymond return the dirt to cover Popcorn's casket. It was then it hit me, like a sledgehammer slamming into concrete, that; my Friend was not going to come out and play with me in the morning. I choked, warning me I had to get out of there. Wheeling my chair away, I silently promised myself, and later; Ray; "Never again! Just ain't worth hurtin' like this."

Eighteen days later: A prisoner approached gingerly, holding in his hands a Watch Cap. He opened it to reveal, inside; a tiny gopher, maybe three-four weeks old, his fur sparse; pink skin peeking through. He had been found bleeding, unable to stand without immediately falling back onto his side.

"Hey, brother, I don't know what to do. I can't take care of him."

"Huh? And I can?"

"Man, somebody told me you're the 'gopher-dude'."

Then there was "Oatmeal." Gotta go....I feel a friend nibbling on my toe.

R.I.P POPCORN

"MY AFFAIR WITH "THE WARDEN"

Regaining consciousness, I noticed the familiar silence of total isolation. I turned my head to find something covering my face. I was lying on my stomach, wrists secured tightly together behind my back. My ankles were bound, knees bent until the heel of each foot rested upon my butt, leg irons affixed to my wrist chain. I was "hot-tied", a specialty of the house inside every state prison; I have been confined: California, Oregon and Washington, as well as County Jails and Juvenile institutions.

First it was the thousands of cockroaches attempting to carry me off, and whatever food may have been in the cracks. Then came the rats: I hated rats! I was scared of rats! I listened as they communicated. I felt them bravely scurry over and around me in their quest to satisfy their insistent curiosity. I imagined them asking one another: "Who is this stranger in our house?"

"It is I, the guy who is going to squish you, you little bastards." Actually they were not little, they were big bastards.

I've no idea, when it was, I first began enjoying the company they seemed to be offering; though a few had, not so sociably, bitten me. Becoming convinced each had its own distinguishing personality, I gave them names.

They didn't even bite the same. "Snowball" would chomp down, preferring to take pieces out, of one or the other, of my elbows. "Slow John" would first sniff and tickle me with his whiskers; begin to nibble gently, then give me one good bite and take off. Now "Hog Jaw" was the one I most feared. He took to exploring down, around, and between my legs. I could feel him sniffing my crotch. While he was there I would remain perfectly still, my legs squeezed together as tight as I could get them.

"How's your day going?" I would ask "Sonny, Jr."

He was forever attempting to nuzzle his way under what I had come to reason was a hood entirely covering my head; its hem secured around my neck keeping it from slipping off. At first I thought Sonny, Jr. might squeeze through, making me worry what he might do there, if he felt trapped and began to panic. Came a time he figured out he wasn't going to squeeze in and took to trying to "dig" under; his sharp little claws cutting into my skin. From Hog Jaw, I learned that these guys have a stubborn streak in them, coupled with a determination I had to admire; no matter I had never run into one rat that refused to bite then leave like other self-respecting "meeces".

The bunch of them, I first estimated dozens in number, were to become family. There can be no doubt their presence kept my mind from free-falling into the waiting abyss that threatens every man's sanity, who dares to challenge Deep Seg[1]

Startling me, the shutter opened.

'How long had it been? Two, three, four days? Maybe they'll give me a little water? Something to eat, possibly?

"Earl, what's going on in here?"

"That there is Abbott, Warden. He messed up Mark really bad."

"I damn well know who he is, mister, and what he did to Mark. What I want to know is why he is like that?"

"He messed up Mark, Wa....."

"Get over here and open this cell. Bloom; you release the gate from there, and then come on back over here. How long has he been like this?"

"Shit, Warden, ain't been but a couple of days. Since he messed up Mark, you know - maybe three days."

"Bloom, you and Earl pull him out of there onto the

---

[1] One of usually half a dozen cells hidden inside Solitary Confinements reserved for those most difficult to control, or those that guards just do not like. It is claimed they no longer exist, but they do.

tier."

"Take it easy, you asses!" Warden continued to instruct.

'Could it be someone had arrived who will get me out of this fix?'

I feared the voices were those I'd been imagining after shifting into survival mode. Once I had accepted it was intended I die; that I was not to leave that cell alive; I gave it over to my brain to get me through it. I had not forgotten what George Jackson told those who listened, what they had to do to survive solitary confinement:

"When we languish isolated for long periods of time, if our minds are right; our bodies will take care of themselves. Our minds are the most important. If they are not healthy, we will not survive the experience; not without considerable damage being done. A diseased mind will infect, destroy one's will to continue.

Work it; put it to labor; what is nine times sixty-two? How many minutes in a year? How many seconds? Imagine the inside of your mother's home, remodel it. Go outside, rip up the ugly landscape and put back the most beautiful of all landscapes in the neighborhood. Play chess; take on challenges during all of your awake hours. Pleasure your mind by thinking of the better life you know will come, if you survive. Remember the first time you fell in love, how it felt when you and your girl lay together. Go out onto a lake with family to fish, swim and laugh. Do these things and you will survive to fight another day."

The hood was roughly removed, allowing light so bright, it temporarily blinded me. As bad as it was back there, the air I then began breathing could never have been fresher.

"Abbott? How you doing?"

I flinched from what may have been, after I gave it some thought later, a compassionate touch on my shoulder.

"I'm Warden Cupp, Abbott. There are a dozen or so of my officers here with you and me. What I need to know is, if I have these chains taken off, get you cleaned up, are you going to give us any trouble?"

"Jesus Christ, Warden. I don't think you want to do that. You should see what he done to Mark."
"Earl, you go up and key the gates. Get the hell out of here," Warden Cupp instructed Mr. Potty in his Pants.

"How is it, Abbott?"

"Don't think I could do much if I wanted to, Warden.

Don't much feel like it anyhow." I could manage no more than a whisper.

"Okay, I'll take your word on that. You'll let me know if you do get to feeling like it, won't you?"

"Not a problem."

"Remove the chains. Be careful. Hold on to him. Don't hurt him unless he gets stupid."

"Take it real easy, Abbott. There's been enough problems here. We ain't looking for more. What do you say?"

"Sounds right to me, Warden." I mumbled.

"Easy now, sit him up."

"Sorry, can't feel my legs, my hands, nothing there."

"Get a goddamn medic down here. You best move your fucking ass, Earl."

'Poor Earl.'

It was a matter of minutes, maybe five, before both my hands and feet were experiencing considerable pain. I was trying to think; but was unable to remember how long they had been without circulation. Then it came to me that everyone squatting around me had pretty much relaxed their hold. It's in my nature; I had to think about it.

'I should be able to get a couple before they take me down,' but I was just too weak, hurt too much. Besides, I'd made a promise to this guy, and my word means a lot to me; I've not much else left.

"Here's the water, Mr. Cupp."

"Don't give it to me, you idiot, give it to him!"
"Drink it slow. There's more."

Resisting temptation to gulp it, I sipped from the paper cup, swished the cold, fresh water over the inside of my mouth and swallowed it with a new-found appreciation for the wonders of nature.

"He's dehydrated, smells horrible, needs a shower and something to eat," shared the medic. "He needs some sutures on the back of his head and his face. Those I can deal with here in the office. Nose too, if he wants."

"Abbott, you want me to straighten your nose? If not you will never be pretty again. It'll hurt like hell, but I'm thinking you're kind of used to that."

"Go ahead," I dreaded. He reached over, grabbed it

between his fingers and was done! I heard it; damn sure felt it, and would have yelped had I not been trying so hard to be hard.

"It'll heal, actually rather quickly. Other than what I've listed, best I can figure he'll be fine. You got yourself a tough one there."

"Okay. Get his hand 'cuffed in front. Help him to the shower; get him cleaned up, clothes, something to eat. Then give him over to Christian so he can stitch him up.

"How you feel about that, Abbott? We still on the same page?"

"No problems today. Can't predict tomorrow," I truthfully answered him.

"I can respect that. Get him to the shower."
"Earl; Bloom; the whole damn bunch of you, as soon as I can get your reliefs in here I want you in my office."

'Poor Earl.'

I completed my shower, during which I had carefully soaped over the many huge dark bruises, long angry looking scratches and bites. I made no effort to estimate their number. Through the barred, locked shower gate, I was handed clean underwear and socks. Wrists again 'cuffed' together, this time behind my back; I was taken into a room where the medic; Christian, was seated at a large conference-like table. Laid out before him were the supplies he needed to fix me, physically. I refused Novocain, not out of bravado, but paranoia. I had no idea what was in that syringe and had no intention of finding out.

I directed his attention to the five more serious wounds I had felt with my hands in the shower: two of them on the back of my head, one above my left eye, a nasty gash on my forehead and another on my chin. Everything else, I concluded, would eventually heal without his help.

"I brought you antibiotics. You need to take two, four times a day for three days, and drink a lot of water. I'm going to put four into your mouth to take before you leave. They said that would be okay, so let's hope they don't take them."

"The water is out, doc."

"Dealt with, as you will see, when you get back to your cell. Warden took care of that. Sorry I can't do any more, Abbott." I believed him. Seemed like a decent guy.

For whatever reason, I was not again to see Warden Cupp, nor another shower for that matter. I would detect a change in how I was treated, or not treated, depending upon what side of the bars one was viewing events from.

While being escorted to the back by half dozen or so guards, I felt eyes of the curious and heard whispered words of encouragement from the shadows.

"A man, with reason to fear he would violently be violated, once announced to his enemies: 'I would rather die on my feet than to live upon my knees! To approach fear on any other level is turning your existence over to anyone who demands it of you!'

For that outburst I was charged 24 antibiotic capsules, the small plastic bag snatched from my hand as I entered the cell.

Before the light was shut out, I was surprised to discover the floor clean and dry. The moldy blanket had been replaced. To the side of the door, on the floor, was a capped, metal pitcher filled with fresh water, small enough to fit through the slot in the door, large enough it could not be slipped through the bars into the cell.

This respite gave me opportunity to do what had not been done before, because of the circumstances, impossible. Every convict knows one of the very first things he must do upon entering an assigned cell for the first time is to methodically and meticulously search it. After feeling over the most obvious areas, such as the underside of the bars, I began to slowly move my fingertips lightly over the walls, every square inch I could reach. I am looking for contraband a prior tenant might have squirreled away.

Weapons, weapon stock, and other, smaller, items accumulated and regarded as contraband inside prison must be hidden. Considering cells are routinely searched, those contraband items not intended for use in the immediate future must be safely stored long term. Probably the most ingenious is to laboriously scrape concrete from a wall, often using the very weapon stock we intend to hide, and construct a cavity whatever size is required. Sealed in plastic wrapping, the item(s) are then placed inside the hollow.

Bars of soap are soaked in water for several days to produce a putty-like substance. With it we fill and smooth over the cavity, sealing in the contraband. A pack of cigarettes will buy a tin of primer and matching wall paint to brush over the soap. After several coats, sometimes having to repaint the entire wall, or cell, once dry the work becomes invisible. Only by feel could it thereafter be located.

More often than one might think, these caches are left undisturbed for long periods. A convict originally laboring over a project will, for one reason or another, be removed from his cell and taken to a place where he cannot after return to retrieve what he has stashed. Personally, I have never found one, but I know others who have, most recently; guards poking around with their portable, hand-held metal detectors.

So began four and a half years. I would never again be chained and left hanging from the bars, nor would I be made to lie like an abused dog in its own waste. Other than that, nothing changed.

From time to time I would be given my shower, via the fire hose, usually after words were exchanged and I invited them to come on in. Never did I speak from loneliness; I have my mouses for those times. They were much more intelligent than my keepers, and great company.

Whenever I said something to the guards, there was a method to my madness, as the saying goes. Usually it was the stink in the cell. When it became more than I cared to deal with, I would make unflattering remarks about their manhood and suggestive comments about their mothers. They would respond with curses, discuss my mother, and give me a bath. The rats knew when I raised my voice it was time for them to leave and they were gone like a shot.

I suppose at some point we both knew it was just a game we played with one another, the guards and me.

For sure we all knew neither of us was going to do anything, regardless of how many times we killed the other with our mouths. There were days upon which I had to be more vigilant than others. Wednesdays, for instance, there were two exceptionally sneaky guards. I didn't want the rats harmed, and if I was not holding my, once again, moldy and rotting blanket in front of me, keeping the powerful jet of water from hitting me straight on, I would be hurt. Won some, lost some.

With each new week my situation became less difficult to deal with. Unfortunately; however, 'hopelessness' settled in. This is a consequence that is inevitable. No matter the battles won, and lost, there, every man, woman and child entering solitary confinement will leave permanently psychologically and emotionally damaged. There is absolutely no possibility they will survive unscathed. In the end it is but a matter of measure.

Through the years I was OSP, struggling to hold onto whatever I could of my sanity, there were a number of things I did that many, understandably, would view, at best, as strange. Others would no doubt become convinced I had to be straight-up crazier than a bedbug. Don't ask; I have no idea how crazy a bedbug is.

I've no doubt; most of us have been told it's okay to talk to yourself; but, when you begin answering your own questions, you have a problem, or something like that. Should that philosophy be correct; then I am no doubt quite disturbed; considering the hundreds of long, two-way conversations I shared with family members and other folks I would summon up with my imagination.

Along with my imagined characters, I would short-step in circles around the cell acting out different skits conceptualized in my mind.

I was famous, had a wonderful life, everyone was proud of me: I was a hired gun, the fastest throughout the West; a bank robber who gave his spoils to beloved family.

Sonny's Artwork

I resisted nothing that was promised to take me from the enveloping darkness. I'm sure a psychotherapist would make a lot of this. It is what they do, offer fancy labels. But I am convinced it saved me, and I thank George Jackson for sharing his insight with all of on the tier with him at San Quentin.

Ruchell Magee, the only prisoner who would survive the Marin County Courthouse killings. Later he would join with George Jackson in the Adjustment Center killings of two guards and three inmates.

Meant to do nothing more than sustain life, with rare exception, for breakfast I would be given a small paper bowl of oatmeal cereal and a half pint of milk, except on Monday when I would be given, in addition, a pastry, and on Sundays one fried egg atop my oatmeal. These two days, Mondays and Sunday, I used, or tried, to keep track of the other days. Lunch consisted of a bologna sandwich soaked in mustard, served on a paper plate. Depending upon which guard brought it to me, I might be given an orange or an apple. Rarely, sometimes two pieces of fruit. Dinner was my favorite. There would be two slices of fresh brown bread laid atop a medium sized paper bowl half filled with what I thought of as *goulash*. It was surprisingly tasty and, I believe, nourishing, with its meat and assorted vegetables I could feel floating in delicious, thick, dark gravy.

Succumbing to curiosity, once when I was sipping from the bowl, each sip became *one tablespoon*. There were thirty-four. I had planned, 'when I get out of here' to see how much that was, but I never did.

Along with breakfast and dinner, the pitcher would be exchanged. Always fresh and cold, I could easily pour the water from it through the bars into my paper cup. All in all it could have been worse. It could have been better.

When I first arrived at OSP and had to relieve myself, before the guards took a serious dislike to me, I urinated laying flat over the hole in the floor. The other option would have been to stand and hope the stream went where it was meant to. I heard a *squeak* inside the hole and frantically withdrew; thinking of the possible consequence should a mouse take an interest in me about that time. Since a small boy, I was afraid of rodents after a field mouse bit me on the left eyelid. Mama, not having raised a fool, though I suspect many would argue that; I did not hesitate to begin peeing in my cup and pouring its contents down the drain.

I cannot accurately share how long I had been there, a year, likely more, possibly less, before I made friends with one of the many dozens of sewer rats visiting me all hours of the day and night. It was an activity I encouraged by attempting to always have bits of food out on the floor. They appeared to particularly favor the apples, stale bread and carrots I would share from the goulash. I was not sure what they thought of the oranges.

My unreasonable fear of the critters had stilled during the times I was hog-tied. Afterward, looking for a friend, I would sit, legs crossed, place the back of each hand flat onto the concrete floor and splay my fingers. A piece of fruit in the palm of one hand, bread in the other, I would patiently wait, sometimes hours. I could not see them crawling over me, but I was able to discern most were large in body, some heavier than others. I learned quickly if I didn't move in a manner that frightened them they would not bite me. Collectively they made so much noise; squeaking and doing what it is that rats do; I became concerned should a guard stand at the front of the cell, and I not be aware of him; he would clearly hear them through the door. But, thinking it over, I doubted the bulls would act out of concern; well, maybe for the rats.

'You little fellas need to hold down the racket. Don't want the pigs to know you're here with me.'

I was relieved to find that when I spoke in a sharp, urgent tone of voice they would stop, instantly become quiet, and return to what they were doing only after deciding whatever danger may have existed was no more. Other than the fact they were choosing to live inside a Deep-Seg prison cell, I found nothing at all stupid about them.

My patience would eventually be rewarded by a particularly brave soul that began taking time to sniff at my hand. I would feel his wet little nose and fluttering whiskers tickle whichever hand he had approached, before snatching the food and running off. Some days later he began resting his paws on my palm. Within a week, instead of doing a drive-by, he remained and had his meal laying half on and half off of my palm, his teeth harmlessly scraping across my skin. Whenever I lay on the floor wrapped in my blanket, he took to sniffing my chin, nose, eyes and at my hairline. After many foiled attempts, I reached out and was allowed to touch him, feel his harsh hair. Then he bit me.

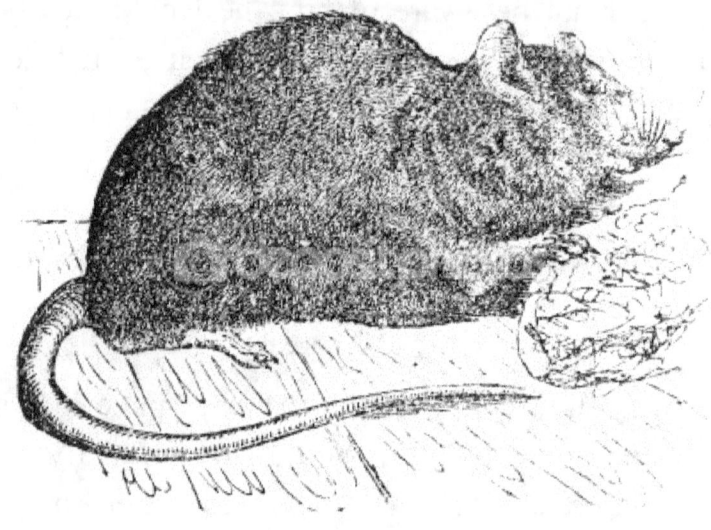

"Ouch, you little fucker. What did you do that for?"

"Because that's what I do when people get too close."

"I can relate to that."

I drifted to sleep listening to the scampering and frolicking of my many associates. I felt his whiskers tickling my ear. I had no idea which of us was more brave, as I slowly and carefully reached out and touched his long, thick tail. I felt it stiffen and then relax when I did not jerk my hand away. By night's end; what I thought to be night; I was gently scratching his back with one fingernail while he nudged against my face. When we were not doing that; with his paws, he would play with my hair. I wondered if *he* was a *she,* possibly seeking to build a nest ?

There was no way I could know if "Warden" would leave and come back, or if he remained and lived solely on the food I provided. Attempting to feed them all, I doled out half my rations, of which Warden got a good chunk. What I did know; whenever I was awake, even if I had just awakened, he was sure to be nearby. If I made any sound with my mouth, he would be there in seconds, nuzzling me.

Whenever the door slot was opened for my food to be shoved through and the trash removed, there would be just enough light I could see the last of my mouse's butts as they scrambled back down the hole. I've always wondered how so many were able to disappear so quickly at once. During these interruptions, Warden had taken to running under the blanket and attempting there to burrow into my armpit, or between my legs.

Once we decided we could be friends I began an attempt to take it to the next level. The first weeks, each time he felt my hand lightly on his back, he would wiggle out from under.

"What's wrong, Big Guy? Something get hold and hurt you?"

"I'm being a rat, silly."

It thrilled me when he finally allowed me to pick him up. He was much larger than I had thought, and obese. In fact, Warden was frikking huge, similar in size to that of an average sized cat. I became concerned he may have eaten himself out of any chance to escape back down the hole should he have to. 'Maybe that is why he took to hiding under the blanket?' I questioned myself.

"Going to have to put you on a diet, Warden. What would happen to you when they come and take me somewhere else? You and I both know they are going to do that someday, right? They are mean people. They would come in here and hurt you real bad, and enjoy it," I cautioned him.

"Abbott, listen up. Looks like we have a sewer rat epidemic in the cell block. They're coming through the toilets here on the first floor. Think you could behave yourself if I gave you a trap?"

"I got no mouse problem in here," I answered as a dozen or so hugged against my legs, shivering. "I ain't seen one since I arrived. I'll let you know if I do."

"Suit yourself."

"Hey, asshole, you in there? I got your mother here with me." I knew that voice but was unable to put a face with it, at first.

"Got a little something for you to remember me by." It was "Mark".

"Been a while, piglet; no way I'll forget. Every time I hear a stick snap in half I'll think of you."

The shutter was opened. I grabbed my blanket and knelt so I would not be knocked down. As I moved to hold it up in front, the water slammed into my chest, forcing all the air from my lungs. At the same time, my body was propelled backward, across the floor, where I hit the wall with my head; hard!

"You're going to die in there; you know that; right, Abbott? Too fucking bad I won't be around to enjoy watching that happen. Adios, motherfucker."

"You still sucking through a straw, tough guy?"

After, I sat and listened to his keys jingle off. I had no memory of the water ever being that powerful before. I suspected old Mark had attached one of those adjustable nozzles on it just to tell me goodbye. The guy was quite a piece of work. Far from the exception, during my many years of incarceration inside youth and penal institutions, I have often run into guards like him; torturing and brutally assaulting helpless prisoners.

"Well, Warden, things had been a little too quiet around here. What you think?"

I stood to hang my blanket. It would be a few days before it was dry enough to wrap myself in. I began pushing water toward the hole so I'd have a dry floor to sleep on.

"I'm not sure how much more of this I want to take, Warden. It has to be a couple years no, huh? We going to make it or what?"

Remembering there was a strong possibility Warden could not fit down the hole, wishing I had put him on the diet he needed, I began feeling around for him; first the blanket, then over the floor.

"Where you at, mouse? You can't fit your fat ass down that little hole, can you?"

"You got nerve calling my ass fat. Don't forget that I can see yours, convict."

"Yeah, yeah, run your mouth, Warden, or whatever that thing you eat with is called. You know I had hold of your ass, and for sure if I could see it when you walk, it would look like two wild cats fighting inside a burlap bag. Every heard that one before, mouse?"

"So, you're a perv now, feeling me up? By now you gotta be thinking I'm kinda fine, huh?"

All the while he and I discussed his rear end I was moving my hands over the floor. When I brushed against fur, hair, whatever one might wish to refer to it as, I knew it had to be Warden. Thoroughly wet, he did not move when I lifted him from the floor. I placed my damp hand near his nose and found he was not breathing. Warden was dead. I felt my heart begin to skip beats, fluttering, as his whiskers once had.

I have no idea how it happened, not exactly. In my mind I went over the events. Holding Warden in my hand, I physically acted out everything that had happened during those minutes. I had been lying down, playing with Warden. Hearing the pig's voice he scampered off and I stood up. When the shutter opened I knelt down, grabbed hold a piece of the blanket and yanked it up to hold in front of me. I failed to think of Warden habitually running to cover himself in it whenever he perceived danger was lurking. Could be I shook him from it, or he had been holding on and the water knocked him off.

Either way, there was no place else for him to go other than across the floor and into the hole. It had to be at that moment the water crushed his little body, or I stepped on him.

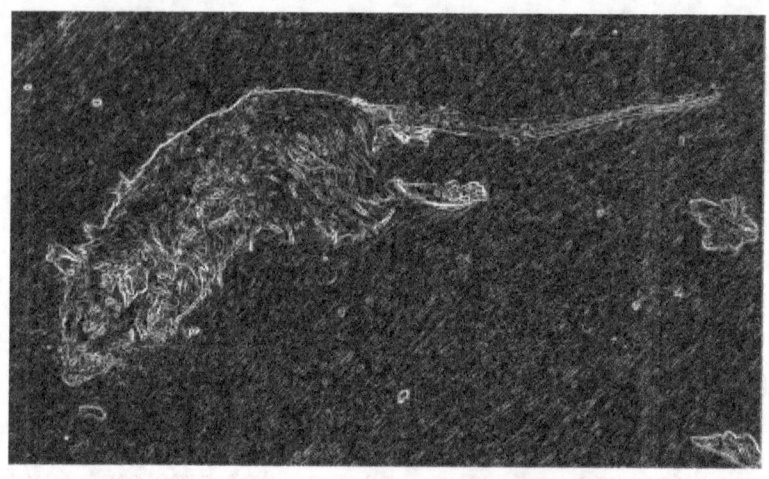

I sat, Warden now held in both my hands. Tears threatened. He didn't feel so big anymore. We had been together nearly eighteen, twenty-four months? He had been my life preserver, my friend. A sewer rat kept me going when I didn't want to, and nobody else cared if I did. I've thought long and hard about it and there is no way I can explain how this mutual friendship came about, nor describe how very real it was and felt. I would have died protecting him had I been given that choice. Warden led me to understand being an *animal*, as my keepers refer to me, is not such a bad thing. Much worse is being human.

"I'm sorry, buddy, really sorry. I guess you shouldn't have trusted me after all, just like you first figured. I got you killed. On my skin, mouse, I promise if that piece of shit ever gets close enough I'll kill him!"

After Warden's death I gave no attention to the days passing. No longer did I care to count them, or to know if it was Sunday or Monday. I continued my interest in the rats visiting and eating the food I left out, which became the majority of my rations, but it was not to be the same again. I never again spoke aloud to them, or to myself. I said nothing to the guards who were apparently satisfied I was there, breathing, each time they removed the empty paper place or bowl I set near the door slot.

Warden's death had left me emotionally devastated. Much more so than when I had been kidnapped, transported illegally across state lines, and placed inside Deep-Seg solitary confinement. Unlike the loss of Warden, I got over the fact they did this without benefit of legal representation as guaranteed by the United States Constitution to **all** people on American soil, under its control and/or in its custody and care.

I assumed because I was no longer discussing their mothers sexual preferences and habits, the guards lost their motivation to shower me. My long hair became so thickly matted with filth I could no longer run my fingers through it. To entertain myself I would scrape the caked dirt from my face and arms where there were now sores from which I obsessively picked off the scabs. I had torn from my underwear a strip of cloth with which to wipe clean what teeth were left after I was beaten. Pieces, of those broken, would occasionally work their way out of my gum and give me some relief, but there was always pain. The rotten taste permeating my mouth was a constant reminder my dental hygiene had not been par for some time.

Thoughts of suicide came, they went; convinced it was one of but two options available to me. The other was to close my eyes and slip silently off into another darkness, that of insanity. 'Would I be happy there? Prisons serving as warehouses for the mentally ill; I've met many *crazy people* who appeared anything but *happy*.'

Rabi Nahman Emerson wrote: "If you won't be better tomorrow than you were today, then what do you need tomorrow for?" It was a question I had begun to ask myself more and more.

When a child, no one listened to my cries for help, as I related in my book: "I Cried, You Didn't Listen". My pleas were for someone; anyone, to rescue me from those entrusted to care and watch over a nine year old boy; not beat and rape me.

Here I am still; now living the aftermath, older, wiser,

incarcerated with the big boys, buried inside Deep-Seg and still experiencing man's inhumanity. Nothing has changed, other than; now it is even more certain; no one is listening.

Snowball[2] had been the realist. Somehow he had seen what lay ahead and decided he wanted not to be a part of it. 'All I have to do is join him', I thought to myself. 'Climb those bars as high as I can go and drop head first onto the concrete. That should do it. What if it didn't? What if I screw that up; like I have everything else in my life?' The blanket was not an option. It was so rotted it wouldn't hold the weight of someone suffering through the last stages of anorexia nervosa. 'When am I going to make a decision? Am I? Can I? What if.....?

---

[2] Snowball, the man, was my cellie at San Quentin Prison. Snowball, the sewer rat, was his namesake. You can find the fate of Snowball, the man, written in CONSEQUENCE.

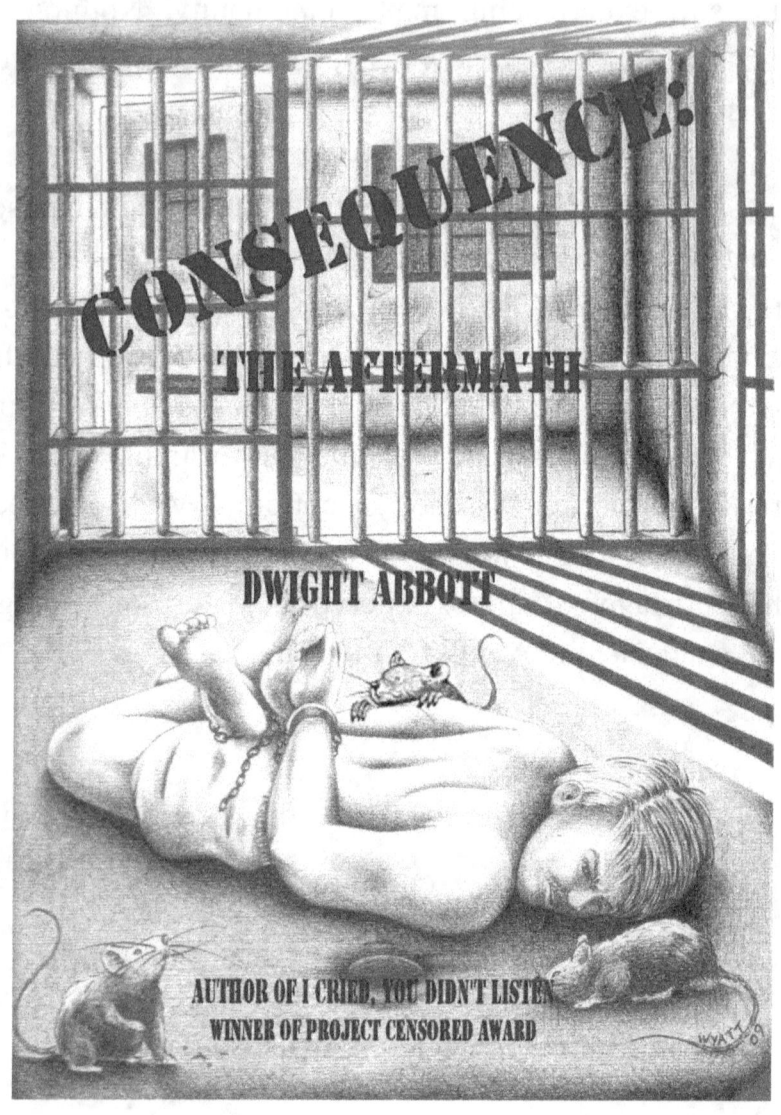

SAN QUENTIN

Prison of heartaches, anguish and tears,
where there is no hope, only fear,
I despise.
This graveyard for many,
this shame on all,
where I exist,
back unbent, standing tall,
I despise
Fortress of madness and frustration,
bastions filled with untold pain,
I challenge again, again, again!
I dispute your authority
over my life, my soul,
hidden behind fungus covered granite walls,
smelling of spattered blood and mold.
Your foundation of rock and steel were laid
by sadists long gone;
your torch kept burning
by Devil's spawn.

Fuck you, your threats,
oppression, solitary cells and greed,
enough of my blood you have let.
I promise, a day will dawn,
upon which alarms will toll,
The Reaper has come to collect
for the senseless destruction of souls.
As sure as the Eagle takes flight,
vengeance will resound,
taken by men
whose lives and souls you bound.
I'll savor my moment,
you sadistic whore!
Knowing a "moment" is all I'll have,
before a bullet takes me to the floor.
Ah, what the hell, San Quentin,
I'm too old, far too much blood has flowed,
I'll give you what you would not,
mercy instead of a show . . .
Naught!

Dwight Abbott, 2009

The Sun-Telegram

Sunday, November 28, 1976   San Bernardino County

ESCAPE — Dwight Edgar Abbott II, 34, of Soledad State Prison. Charged with escape from state prison. Pleaded guilty as charged. Sentence to state prison suspended, ordered to serve one year in county jail with credit for 124 days already

SOLEDAD STATE PRISON

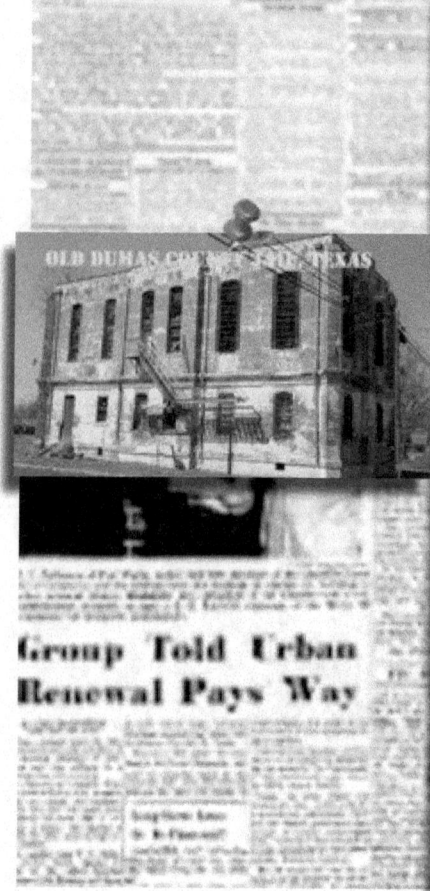

AMARILLO GLOBE-TIMES
Final Edition

Wednesday, July 20, 1960   Amarillo, Texas

Man Escapes Dumas Jail

DUMAS, July 20 (Special) — Moore County officers and Dumas police continued their search today for a pipeline worker who escaped from the Dumas jail through an air shaft about 4 p.m. Tuesday, although no new developments had been reported in the search this morning.

The worker was arrested for creating a disturbance and for investigation in connection with another offense. He is Dwight Edgar Abbott, 21.

Police first learned of the escape, according to Dumas Police Chief Frank Hudson, when a man in the apartment house where Abbott had been living reported the escapee had rushed into his apartment for a butcher knife and then left.

Abbott was described as about 6 feet tall, weighing about 175 pounds and wearing a duck-tail haircut. His hair is a straw brown.

Group Told Urban Renewal Pays Way

CONTACT SONNY

If you wish to contact Sonny, you may write to him
at:
Dwight Abbott T-88033
California Health Care Facility
P.O. Box 32200 C-3A-101
Stockton, Ca. 95213-2200

<u>SKIPPY'S CONTRIBUTIONS</u>

I have asked my brother, if he would like to share some of what few moments we had together before we 'parted'. The following stories were written by him as part of; 'Our Wrap'!

Danny and Dwight Abbott
[Skippy and Sonny]

The following memories have stayed with me; (Skippy) all my life. I always admired my older brother and still do; no matter how 'far apart' we drifted; no matter where our choices led us.

THE ROCK

By Danny Abbott - Skippy

Preface:

So how long will this take and why am I doing it...? Would I read or even listen to a story of my grandfather's childhood..? Bear with me for a moment, as I think as a child: 'My life is now; not yesterday. I am a busy living, **now,** child, with important and urgent; places to go; people to see and things to do. Who really cares and what real difference will somebody else's old vague story make in the breath I breathe; especially an old story from an old life.'

It is my hopeful prayer of the fact that children may not all think like the above; all their lives; that moves me to write; yet, another story of my childhood; in the thought that one of my children; grandchildren; or beyond; will someday wish to satisfy a curiosity about a, no longer available; older family member. It is uneasy for me to say: "I love you" and think it means something, as words alone; tend to, blow away with the wind.

This and my other stories; boring or not; must now suffice to be my "mi culpa" at the same time it is my "I love you" to BOTH those; I found hard; and those I found easy to love; no matter how late; it took me to say it or show it; even if beyond the grave. Please forgive the pride of my lips and heart. My pride DID and does, hurt me deeply and leaves me regretting my life long 'aloofness'.

And now: **<u>"The Rock".</u>**

Our family spent a lot of my, Reid's; Carolyn's; David's; and Sonny's childhood vacations, if not all, at a place called Willow Beach. It is (was) a remote "resort" nestled next to a meandering bend in the Colorado River. It is a mile or two down river of Hoover (Boulder) Dam on the Arizona side. The Dam itself defines the border between Nevada and Arizona. The dam backs the river into a Lake called "Mead". Lake Mead was, many times, part of our trips to Willow Beach.

Most of our trips required a passage over the dam along with stories, from my siblings, of those many hapless workers who were working on the dam, when 'fate and clumsiness swallowed them up'. The ever growing horrific scenes were intricately described with much drama and animation, by our three older siblings, to a shivering Sonny and myself. It seems that, when the pouring of the concrete was started and the massive buckets were being guided from the side of the canyon to the dam; one or more hapless souls would lose his grip and fall silently; except for his own screams; into the thick wet concrete.

Of course 'rescue' was somehow impossible, because of the difficulty; danger and slowness involved in retrieving a panicked screaming worker from certain death, as the poor soul slowly sank, or was sucked, into the quicksand like sludge. In many cases the buckets were moving so fast, as to bury the worker before he had a chance to sink or let out a second scream that just became a "gurgle"!

Driving over Hoover Dam.

As we drove over the dam; both Sonny and I fearfully felt the mournful calls of these "entombed spirits"; to 'remember' their sacrifice. As a result, we remained silent; our feet no longer resting on the car floorboards; feeling an ever-growing urgency to exit the other side of the Dam, as our peers gleefully chattered on with ever growing tales.

Once safe and sound over the dam; with deep; yet, hidden- not wanting to display fear to our siblings- sighs of relief heightened by being allowed to; once again, rest our aching legs and feet on the floorboards and breath again; we turned our attention to the upcoming turn off to

Willow Beach Arizona.

The turn-off to Willow Beach was another source of excitement, as it was little more than a narrow gravel turn off heading out into a hot dry desert. The first sibling to 'call it' held a momentary pinnacle of high esteem and gratitude from the others. On more than one occasion, dad drove right past it, as he always drove faster than most heroes.

Willow Beach, as seen from the Highway turnoff.

The drive down that dusty dirt road always took longer than it actually was; yet, the reward of finally arriving at the opening scene of; where we were to spend the next few days of our youthful lives, was indescribably delicious. And sometimes, we were immediately rewarded with a wild burrow obstinately blocking our path until we popped the top off a bottle of soda and let him or her chug it down on their own!

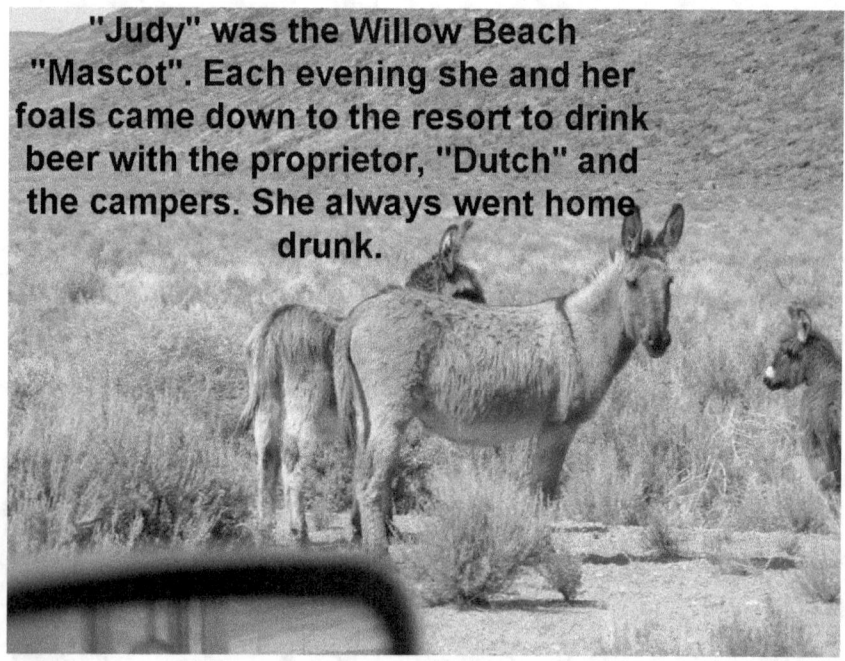

"Judy" was the Willow Beach "Mascot". Each evening she and her foals came down to the resort to drink beer with the proprietor, "Dutch" and the campers. She always went home drunk.

We pulled into a small canyon off the road to the left. This off road was even less than the main dirt road! It was a primitive campground with the less then dirt road access down the middle of the canyon running down to the river.

Along both sides of this road were hollowed out dirt camp pads backed against the rather steep sides of the canyon walls. We took one on the east side. The 'campground' appeared sparsely populated with some small camp trailers and tents. The camp trailers received longing looks from those who normally sleep in cars and/or on outside army surplus dark brown cots; brought home by my army brother; Reid.

Immediately upon parking and exiting the car; the cat and mouse game would begin. If we could escape fast enough; before our parents realized we were gone, camp setup became a 'breeze'! We were all avoiding eye contact, as we quickly began to find interesting things much further away from the camp. Sonny and I could hear the car being unloaded by our whining siblings and order barking parents, as we headed up the west side of the steep canyon beyond the few small trees surrounding the camps in the gully; toward The Rock.

Two small boys on a trek to adventure, scrambling up a tall mountain, simply to discover what was to be seen from the top. Excitement filled our bodies as adrenalin flowed. Small squirrels and lizards scampered from us; hiding on the sparse treeless landscape in crevices and under rocks. On our journey to the top we would move small rocks to the side; seeking these fugitives from curiosity. Spiders, centipedes, scorpions and stranger creatures seemed to abound. A new discovery waited under every rock and patch of dry grass.

We called to each other whenever we made a most 'unusual' find. We would chatter to one another explaining the presence and finer details of what we knew nothing about. We climbed further and further up; occasionally looking back down at the shrinking campsites, and their contents; marveling at how 'small' they were all becoming. We eventually reached the shoulder of the mountain and rested there, while congratulating ourselves for overcoming the steeper part of the Canyon to get where we were. It seemed that, one must be very careful walking along the shoulder or he might fall over the edge and tumble uncontrollably back down into the camp site.

As we scrambled along; forgetting our cares and looking forward to bigger and better surprises, out of the corner of my eye it darted. I am not sure what I saw; yet, when I looked in the direction of the dart, I saw the subject of this story. There sitting serenely upon the shoulder of this mountain was a very large boulder. It was different than the others I had seen.

It spoke to me! It said: "come over here and check me out; notice my size and unusually round shape."

I went over to it. And sure enough; it was big; unique; and reeked of strength! I envied its massive presence on that mountain.

Suddenly I heard it issue a challenging statement: "you will never see what (darted?) is under me cause I am much too big for your puny body to move!"

I was OK until I heard "puny"! I also was

unconsciously sizing up the 'weaknesses' of my 'foe'. True; The Rock was BIG; however, it was round and not sunk too deeply in the hard soil.

I called to my brother: "Sonny; I think I saw something go under this rock; I am going to look."

Back came the 'straw that broke the camel's back': "that rock is too big; you can't move it."

With that; I leaned against its smooth warm resisting surface and pushed. It did not budge. It was, as if, I was not there at all! I leaned harder and pushed. I backed up as far as I could while keeping my hands on the rock and slammed my entire body against it!

Did a feel a slight shudder?

Sonny said: "Let's go!"

I replied: "Come give me a little help; I almost have all the strength I need!"

Sonny begrudgingly came over.

I said: "help me push; it is almost ready to move!"

Sonny and I pushed. The Rock moved a little. Keep pushing I yelled! The Rock shuddered and began to move. We jammed a smaller rock in the crevice produced by its first movement. It could not now fall back. From that position, we pushed it again. It finally rolled over exposing the treasures it thought it could keep hidden underneath. Victory was mine! I felt like superman!

My victory was short lived. The Rock rolled again and then again! It was slowly rolling down the shoulder; yet, slowly gaining speed, as it rolled! At first; it was 'cool'! And then the Rock broached the edge of the shoulder. That was even cooler! As we peered down the steep slope of the canyon, the massive boulder was going full blast with bouncing jumps of 20 feet in the air.

Suddenly it was, as if all life slowed to 'slow motion'. It was then that Sonny and I both instantaneously realized what was going to happen. That Boulder was headed straight for the campground below and directly in its path was the largest camp trailer on the grounds!

My stomach twisted around my neck. I choked at the totally unstoppable scene of destruction and tragedy that was about to follow my stupidity. It is said that nobody expects to die; however, my life, as I had lived it to that point, was to end in the next instant. I could not bear to watch any longer! I threw myself onto the dirt and prostrated myself before a God I previously had only a brief acquaintance with. That; being at the side of my bed with my mother saying: "recite after me: now I lay myself down to sleep….etc".

Rivers of Real Tears flowed, as I silently screamed the first Real prayer of my young life: "Please God; do not allow this to happen to the lives of me; much less; those poor people down there!" Unfortunately; I surmise the prayer was mostly for my own selfish life.

I waited for the crashing sounds of the

boulder hitting and splintering the trailer into a million bits along with the terrible screams of its victims! Yet;, all I heard was a loud gasp of air coming from my brother's lips and then total silence! For a moment, I could not bear to ask what his eyes had seen. I peeked up at him through my tears. He was looking down at the camp and his face was incredulous; his eyes as wide as saucers!

Fully knowing the very worst; Yet hoping beyond any reasonable hope; I hoarsely sputtered: "what happened?". He replied in a breathless gasp: "It stopped!"

I knew it had 'stopped.'!

What do you mean "stopped"; not really wanting to hear the details; yet, wanting to get my life over with quick.

Sonny Replied again; his voice a deep resonating mixture of disbelief and awe: "I told you; It JUST stopped; it was rolling and it stopped!

I said: "what did it hit to stop it?"

He replied: "Nothing; it is just sitting there."

I slowly rose; walked to the shoulder edge and looked over the side. There sitting on a mostly vertical slope about 200 feet up from the trailer; sat The Rock. We both could see nothing around it; and in fact we could make out its full under rounded shape, front and back. Now; I had a look of disbelief and awe. I also could feel the cold beads of vaporizing sweat; relieving my body of 'premature death'. We gingerly made our way down to The Rock. We did not approach it, as we could clearly see that the slightest touch or vibration could start it rolling again!

We ran to our parents and the campers and warned them of the rock. Soon people were swarming to move themselves and their property out of its possible path. We did not tell anybody of the part we played in its existing position.

After all property and people were moved, the rock was simply touched and dramatically; yet harmlessly, continued its "Interrupted" trek.

I visited Willow Beach a few years back. The Rock still lies in this abandoned campground today, as a reminder of my folly and the Unconditional Deliverance of the Lord. Sonny and I stole Our King's Glory on that day; even as, we hid our own sin. Today I attempt to return Our King's Glory, while revealing my own sin.

The "Rock"

So My Progeny take an example and pass on to your own progeny what Great Things the

Lord has Done for you; because He Has! But don't ask me: "Why?" XXOO, Dad.

THE JACKET

BY

DANNY ABBOTT

What was it in those days? I was 13 years old and Sonny was 14. He had been gone for a long time and I did not quite know where he was. I missed him and thought of him, but my parents avoided 'too much' conversation, whenever, I brought it up. The most common one sentence answer; I got, was: "He is staying with Carolyn [our half-sister]." I did not understand why; however, the answer reassured me he was being taken care of and must have wanted to be where he was. The few times I overheard a few phone calls he made to Dad; my dad would always seem to say: "you cannot come back here". At the time; it confused and upset me that my dad would not allow Sonny to come back; let alone, just 'visit'..?

In my ignorance, I did not realize; nor even begin to comprehend that Sonny, at 14 years of age, was an escaped fugitive from the law. To this day, 60 years later; I still cannot comprehend it; nor think of it, without feeling a great deal of pain; physically and emotionally. I still morn the childhood 'loss' of my brother.

As a growing almost teenage boy; my hero, and my friends hero, at that time was James Dean of "Rebel without a cause" fame. James was very similar; yet much more serious, to the Character "Fonzie"; who came much later in "Happy Days".

We all wanted a "Leather Jacket" to sling over our bright white "T-shirts." Each cotton T-shirt having an empty 'Marlborough' hard cigarette pack rolled carefully at the end of its sleeve laying; yet, protruding, from our 'imagined massive bicep'. The jacket was to be left unzipped and ready to remove; easily exposing the rolled pack and bicep, if, and when, a young lady; or peer, might approach. The cigarette tucked carefully, at just the precise angle, behind our ear, was the 'coup de gras', as 'the mark' waltzed, unwittingly, into our man baited, about to spring; inescapable 'trap'.

I had begun asking; begging; my parents for just such a leather jacket, as soon as I noticed my school friends, and enemies, acquiring them. Convincing my parents that; non-withstanding Southern California was too hot for wearing much more than shorts and a T-shirt, my life would be 'over' without that jacket; was no easy task! It could not be just 'any' leather jacket! It had to be a "Genuine Leather" motorcycle jacket; with many bling zippered pockets - for cigarettes and 'switch blades'! Of course, I did not tell my parents the 'real' reasons for all the pockets. The reason being that he, who had the most pockets; and zippered; was the 'Cock of the Walk' with both; his peers AND young ladies! One could notice that even 'enemies' would try to hide a furtive gleam of respect, if they were to menacingly look at you!

It was not long after that my parents 'surprised' me with 'The Jacket'! It was all I had dreamed and more! It had zippered pockets inside and out! It even had zippered sleeves! It was all leather and completely lined to withstand any motorcycle ride in a sub-zero Artic Blizzard! I truly, quickly became known as: "The Jacket"; in school and out! I reeked of James Dean Persona. I was now ready to play the Rebel and defend myself from admiring fans! I even began building my first power converted bicycle - I mean motorcycle!

I was a month or two into the jacket, when I was awakened, from sleep, by a loud commotion going on in our kitchen. At first frightened, I attentively listened. I could hear the voices of my brother, Sonny, and my father. They seemed to be trying to keep their voices to a whisper; yet failing. I heard fear; panic, haste and sadness all at once. My mother was also softly crying. I did not understand.

At last; my brother was home! I wanted to

run to him; hug him; and tell him how much I had missed him! Yet, I sensed I would be intruding on a very important moment; and I did not want to appear 'juvenile'. I walked slowly from my bedroom to the kitchen. I peeked around the corner of the entry. My dad and Sonny were face to face. Sonny was saying he "needed a place to stay"? My dad was saying: "this is the first place they will look"? I did not understand! I was mad at my dad! My mother, crying, with piles of Kleenex in her hands; had not enough to contain her tears. She, seemingly, had 'given up' trying to convince my dad to let Sonny stay?

I noticed we ALL had tears in our eyes!

I had NEVER dared to face off with my dad out of fear and respect. I could hold back no longer; the floodgates opened, as I burst into tears and yelled: "let him stay!" For a moment; one might have heard a pin drop. All eyes were on me. I was scared but stood my ground.

My dad was the first to speak:

"Skippy; you don't understand".

The tone of his voice somehow took me

back from the 'edge of the precipice' upon, which I felt I was standing. My mother, at that moment, rose and gathered me into her arms. Somehow, she coaxed me away from my brother and back to the bedroom. I wanted to hug my brother and tell him I loved him.

In the moments that followed. I remember the background sounds of my Dad and Sonny's continued 'talk'. It sounded, as if; in the distance; they were making 'plans'. My mother; somehow; someway; through her tears, and mine, turned my thoughts from: "My brother MUST STAY here; where he will be loved; safe and protected" to " My brother MUST GO to where he will be loved; safe and protected".

My mom quietly left me to my thoughts and returned to the kitchen. My tears had slowed; yet my heart felt like a large lead weight. Through my tears, I could blurrily see my leather jacket hanging in my closet.

It was dark and rainy outside.

I knew my brother was about to do what I knew, I could NEVER do!

I had fantasized of being the brave; courageous and carefree "Adventurer"; conquering the wilderness with just a knife and a coonskin hat. I had never thought of being 'forced' to do it, with no choice of my own.

I suddenly filled with a sense of dread for my brother! I felt urgency!

I ran to the closet and grabbed "The Jacket". I proceeded to search my memory of all the adventures of Tom Sawyer and Huckleberry Finn; I had ever read. My fanciful plans I had made; came back. I opened ALL the pockets of that jacket and filled them with candy bars; bags of nuts; fruit; flashlight; matches; money; gloves; handkerchief; a hat and my Boy Scout knife.

I could tell by the longer breaks in conversation; and the by increasingly frantic crying of my mother; that the time for Sonny's required departure was quickly nearing. I ran to the kitchen; pushed passed my dad and shoved the; now, very heavy jacket, into a surprised Sonny's arms, and said: "here; take this!" I ran back to my room; afraid that my brother would see my tears and be 'weakened' from the sight!

In the ensuing moments; as the Jacket was quickly perused; I heard both my dad and mom exclaiming: "see here; look you ARE truly loved!" I listened, as the door shut behind my brother.

Author Afterword:

After having feedback from my family about why and how a 14 year old boy could possibly be on the 'lam from the law'; much less supported in that endeavor by his parents; I realized the casual readers of "The Jacket" need one additional piece to this 'puzzle': read Sonny's Book: "I Cried, You Didn't Listen" and you; as I did, will finally; truly understand!

"The Gift"
Dwight Abbott
Karren Killian
1/1/2016

ABOUT THE AUTHOR

Dwight Abbott is currently serving Four 25 year to life; terms at The California Health Care Facility in Stockton. He was raised and trained by the California Youth Authority, from the age of nine. This prepared him to continue his adult life in various penal institutions and penitentiaries throughout California and Oregon. Places include: Preston Castle, Paso De Robles, Deules, San Quentin, Folsom, Salinas Valley State Prison, Pelican Bay and many unmentioned. He is [was] a hardened veteran of the Aryan Brotherhood among others.

He is now an accomplished author of "I Cried, You Didn't Listen" and "CONSEQUENCE", the aftermath.; Both Bestsellers. He recently published a Duology containing both of the above books; Volume 1 and Volume 2 of his Series: "Innocent until 'Made' Guilty". "Innocent until 'Made' Guilty." He maintains his web site at www.DwightAbbott.com. He has joined with his brother, Danny Abbott and other family to co-author "The Serpent Tails".

Dwight's sole remaining Purpose in this life is to have one more young 'rebel' write him and say that Sonny's book had a part in a change of heart; thus avoiding the Path that Sonny took. ALL profits from book sales are returned to the prison inmates through stamps; quarterly packages; phone calls; visitation and incidentals.

AUTHOR POST-DEDICATION

- TO: All the children who shared with me the suffering of physical, mental, sexual and emotional brutality. To those very same boys I met again as an adult, while I served time in Soledad, San Quentin, Folsom and in Oregon state and Washington state penitentiaries.

- To the many I have watched slaughtered on those prisons' yards, and to those who went on to kill - three of whom I wrote to often until they were executed by the state that raised them.

- To all the incarcerated children, who because of cruel physical beatings, sexual molestations and mental manipulations, become society's outcasts and nonconformists; not because they are bad children but because they have become products of the system.

- To the children who are - and will be - growing up as I did, filled with shame and guilt, unable to speak with any member of a society that refuses to lift its head from the sands of ignorance and denial.

- To the future victims of these victims.

- To the following men:

George Jackson, shot and killed by guards at San Quentin; Billy Cook, murdered at San Quentin; Gary Gilmore, executed by the state of Utah; Tony Zamore, murdered at San Quentin; Wallace Michael Ford, murdered at Vacaville; Dennis Dimmick, murdered at Vacaville; Jimmy Trembly, murdered at Soledad; Kenny West, shot and killed during a bank robbery; "Joker" Jones, murdered by prison guards at San Quentin; "Wop", murdered by inmates at San Quentin; Jason, poisoned at Oregon State Penitentiary; and to Charles Manson, a friend whose soul was killed by the System.

- To Silverthorn Resort & Marina and Hidden Valley Market who saved my life and inspired the theme of this book.

- To ALL those above; I dedicate this book.

Dwight Abbott

Read about Sonny's return from the Optmist Home for Boys in
Chapter 5 of "I Cried, You Didn't Listen."
With his Family; 1955; 13 years old..7326 Nestle Ave, Reseda Ca.
Danny (Skippy); halfsister, Carolyn J. Scott; half brother, David L. Scott;
mother, Betty; Dwight (Sonny); dad, Dwight Sr.

Read about Sonny's return from the Optimist Home for Boys in Chapter five of "I Cried, You Didn't Listen". Sonny visits his family at 7326 Nestle Ave. Reseda California. From Left: Danny (Skippy); half-sister, Carolyn J. Scott; half-brother, David L. Scott; mother, Betty (Scott) Abbott; Dwight (Sonny); dad, Dwight Senior.

Sonny's last home
in Redding, Ca

"ON A HILL FAR AWAY"

Karren Killian
Here's Lookin at you
"Kid!"

Skippy & Sonny Abbott; "Brothers Forever!"
Salinas Valley State Prison. Sunday, October 19, 2008.
(Danny O'Neil & Dwight Edgar)

Skippy & Sonny Abbott; "Brothers Forever!"
Salinas Valley State Prison, Sunday, October 19, 2008
[Danny O' Neil & Dwight Edgar]

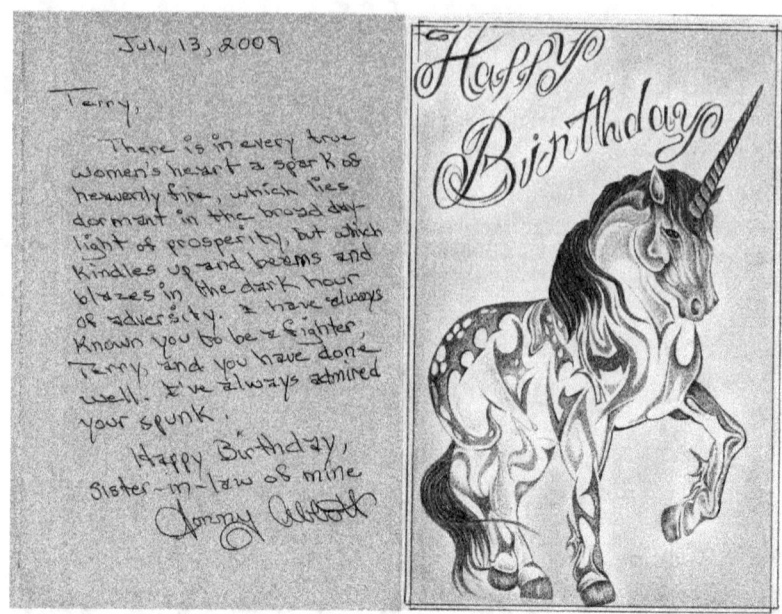

July 13, 2009

"Terry,

There is in every true woman's heart a spark of heavenly fire, which lies dormant in the broad daylight of prosperity, but which Kindles up and beams and blazes in the dark hour of adversity. I have always known you to be a fighter, Terry, and you have done well. I have always admired your spunk.

Happy Birthday,
Sister-in-law of mine

Sonny Abbott

Danny & Terry Abbott
16818 Dog Creek Rd.
Lakehead, California
2004
"Thank You"
By
Dwight Abbott

www.ingramcontent.com/pod-product-compliance
Lightning Source LLC
Chambersburg PA
CBHW072044280526
45788CB00006B/2174